SAILING SMALL CRUISERS

A guide to equipment, safety and seamanship

JC WINTERS

D1059210

Adlard Coles Nautical
London

Published in 1995 by Adlard Coles Nautical
an imprint of A & C Black (Publishers) Ltd
35 Bedford Row, London WC1R 4JH

Copyright © J C Winters 1995

First edition 1995

ISBN 0-7136-3913-X

A CIP catalogue record for this book is available from the
British Library.

Typeset in 10 on 11½pt Memphis Light by Falcon Oast
Graphic Art, Surrey
Printed and bound in Great Britain by The Cromwell
Press, Melksham, Wilts

Contents

Introduction

The enjoyment of any yacht, large or small, depends upon many things – not least of which is how well it is suited to the owner's needs and expectations. These may alter as the years go by with the emphasis being placed upon different attributes, but it would probably be fair to say that the small yacht (defined here as not more than 22 ft (6.7 m) in length overall) would usually be thought of as the first boat – useful for developing the skills of seamanship and navigation. Expectations might well be limited to nothing more ambitious than relaxed daysailing, the occasional club race on Sundays and perhaps, from time to time, a foray along the coast in settled weather. In the normal course of things, this small yacht would be traded for a larger craft, quite probably one with more spacious accommodation and, depending upon the owner's acquired predilection, one with handling characteristics slanted either towards stability and an easy motion at sea or out-and-out performance.

Although there have always been those who understood the attraction of the small yacht – think of the immense popularity of the pocket cruiser of the 1960s – the attractions of the small, or micro, yacht have come to be fully appreciated in recent years. Design has undergone something of a seachange too and the compromise between accommodation and handling characteristics has, arguably, never been better achieved. Performance can be quite exhilarating, even in a boat where the accent is on cruising, for the sense of responsiveness and speed are enhanced by the short waterline length, low freeboard and relatively light weight. Most modern small yachts do prove immensely rewarding to sail – although a different approach is called for at extremes of the wind scale – and the rig and gear are both light and simple therefore within the capabilities of even the younger members of the crew. If the economics of owning a small craft come to mind first, then micros are especially attractive; for moorings, insurance and general outgoings are far lower for a 20 footer than for one of 30 ft (9.1 m) overall. And, since virtually all micro yachts of modern glassfibre or veneer construction are both light and tough, they can be trailed behind a family-sized car; this not only reduces mooring and lay-up costs, but also enables new sailing areas to be explored.

Variations in micro yacht design are many and wide-ranging – arguably, there are more options available than with larger yachts. Some designs place the accent squarely on speed, and these are laid out and equipped solely for competition. Some of these craft encourage a more relaxed attitude and are ideally suited to family pottering and weekend cruising. Yet others are specifically designed and constructed as seagoing vessels with all that that implies. This versatility is in itself an attraction: given shallow or variable draft, micros are not only at home in rivers, estuaries and coastal waters, but they can reach those tranquil backwaters unexplored by larger, deep-draft craft. And although there are a few dissenting voices, there is no doubt that small yachts can safely be cruised offshore – so long as they are built and equipped for this specific purpose, and the crew is both experienced and confident.

Of course, there is nothing new about blue water cruising in small craft. Yachts under 20 ft (6 m) overall have been crossing and re-crossing seas and oceans since records began. And not just cruising, but racing as well; the first recorded single-handed transatlantic race in 1891 seems to have consisted of a duel between two Americans in boats reputed to be no more than 13 ft (3.9 m) overall length. This is not necessarily a practice to be recommended, but it has to be admitted that time after time competently handled small yachts have come safely through storms that carry away the superstructure, sweep the decks and buckle the plates of commercial and naval shipping. (Ironically, it is the sheer numbers of such vessels in coastal waters that arguably pose the single greatest danger to the small yacht – not the size of the seas or the strength of the wind!)

Given the qualities of the best of the genus, many owners of larger vessels come to realise that small is beautiful, and they return once more to cruising or racing in smaller vessels. True, micros hold little appeal for those who share the American perception of a yacht as a 'recreation centre', but for people who appreciate a closeness with the elements, and a harmony with wind and water, the freedom of sailing a small yacht is one of the greatest pleasures life can offer.

1   Definition by Design

What is a micro yacht?

The term 'micro yacht' is an arbitrary one. In fact, it could be argued that it is no more than a trendy 'designer' label for what was popularly called a 'pocket cruiser' a generation or so ago. However, the term is now in current usage, and generally accepted as describing a sailing cruiser with overall length of around 20 ft (6 m), providing overnight or weekend accommodation in a fixed cabin (as opposed to open boats whose crews must rough it on temporary berths under a tent cover). It also presupposes that the vessel will be a seagoing vessel, albeit in miniature.

To this end, the micro yacht would be expected to have a cockpit or footwell affording a measure of security, and that this, if not actually self-draining, would at least be watertight and capable of being bailed or pumped out. (The alternative would be to have a cockpit sufficiently protected so that there would be no likelihood of shipping water.) Decks should have secure toe rails, a non-slip surface, and deck fittings commensurate with the type of sailing and intended cruising area. Obviously this deck hardware must include well-laid-out tracks and leads, cleats and rope stoppers – or winches – to enable the working sails to be easily handled and reefed. If the crew so desires, it should also be feasible to hang up such light-weather sails as a spinnaker, blooper, ghoster or other enticing nylon frippery! Equally important for any craft intending to cruise coastwise or in exposed estuaries is that cleats and fairleads are sufficiently strong to withstand the snatch of anchoring in severe conditions; should the vessel ever be in danger of driving on to a lee shore, then the anchor may be the only chance of salvation.

Last, though not usually least, is the requirement that the accommodation should function at sea as well as in harbour; and to this end, there should be fixed berths, a galley with cooker that can be used with safety when under way (and not all can by any means), and some sort of lavatory – however primitive this may be.

Now, sit back for a moment and contemplate a cross-section of the small sailing cruisers on the market – it will not take you long to realise that strict categorisation is far from easy. Even

The little West Wight Potter, a fraction under 15 ft (4.5 m) in overall length, and just about as small as it is possible for a viable cruiser to be. In skilled hands, several Potters have made quite long voyages, but patience would clearly be an asset to skipper and crew!

an exact upper and lower size limit for the micro yacht is open to debate, since, as anyone who has ever given more than a passing glance at yachts in a marina knows, there are quite husky-looking boats of less than 18 ft (5.4 m) in length and diminutive 24 footers. Once on board, appearances can be just as deceptive. Numerous smaller yachts, especially recent glassfibre light displacement types, give a remarkable sense of space on deck and in the cockpit as well as below decks. Thus, for any given length there are many variables, depending on the type of sailing and sailing areas for which the craft has been intended.

Leaving aside the design of the superstructure for the moment, the hull form of a cruising boat suited to estuary and coastal passage making will differ markedly from a craft where performance is the keynote. Length on the waterline, beam – at deck level as well as on the flotation line – the height of the freeboard and the depth of hull (as opposed to the draft that is measured to include the keel) are all crucial in determining the qualities of any yacht, but are especially critical in the design of a successful micro yacht, for here strength, weight and performance are a finely balanced calculation. And if the boat in question is to be regularly trailed, the hull not only has to be light and rugged enough to withstand the stresses imposed when sailing, but also those differing structural strains to which it will inevitably be subjected during launching or bouncing around the countryside behind a car!

There is also the hard fact of commercial viability to be faced, which is always an unwelcome constraint upon the draughtsman's individual preferences. Economics often lie at the root of many minor and not so minor design flaws. Some of these faults may be in structural details, and only emerge after several years' sailing, while others affect the handling and will manifest themselves during the initial sea trials.

For the purpose of this book, a dividing line must be drawn somewhere. An upper limit of 22 ft (6.7 m) overall length seems appropriate, although it could be argued that the length on the waterline is of greater significance since this bears directly upon the available deck, cockpit and accommodation space. It also governs the maximum speed that can be expected from a hull of normal displacement type – although some brochure writers conveniently tend to overlook this when waxing lyrical about performance!

As far as a lower size limit goes, this seems to be decreasing all the time. The Atlantic has, after all, been crossed from west to east by a 'vessel' that is a whisker less than $5^1/2$ ft (1.7 m) overall. (The word 'vessel' is used advisedly, as any control over the ultimate destination is vested in the prevailing winds and ocean currents rather than in the hands of the crew.) Only 3 ft (91 cm) longer than this is Wren, a chubby little pram dinghy with short cabin and yawl rig. She boasts a single berth, and is – so her designer maintains – quite capable of river and sheltered estuary cruising in careful hands. Common sense, however, would suggest that at an inch or two over 15 ft (4.5 m) overall, the West Wight Potter or the classic gaff-rigged Winkle Brig are just about the minimum size compatible with both satisfactory sailing qualities and any semblance of civilisation below decks. Both these qualities, in any case, are inevitably rather compromised by the size of the yacht. Although a well-finished interior with upholstered berths and backrests does contribute to crew comfort and wellbeing, no micro yacht is going to take top honours for seagoing luxury; and cruising for several days and nights in such restricted space does demand a certain attitude to life not suited to every individual (of course there are those who simply prefer daysailing, or an occasional overnight stopover in fine weather).

Length on the waterline

To return to the important factor of the length on the waterline, this decides the theoretical maximum hull speed attainable by any displacement craft – a speed largely dictated by skin friction, form resistance and the wave-making properties of the hull. Except by surfing, only a lightweight sailboat expressly designed to plane can exceed this waterline length/speed limitation. True planing designs, those with beamy 'shallow-sectioned dinghy type' hulls that have a broad transom and flat run aft allied to fairly deep, narrow fin keels, can certainly notch up very high speeds in a fresh wind (and maintain them too, if driven hard by a nerveless and determined crew). The ride will be exhilarating, but also wet, wild and occasionally verging on the uncontrollable. This can be rather alarming, especially in confined or crowded waters, and the less experienced would be well advised to steer clear of such extreme designs since they demand a firm hand on the tiller – and will repay a momentary lapse of the helmsman's concentration by violent changes in course. Even with the boat reefed right down in a blow, directional stability is not a strong point. The helm can never be left unattended (and will make an autopilot work double time with consequent drain on the batteries). Also, very rarely can such a design be persuaded to lie hove-to – and a cruising boat that will not do so puts additional strain on the crew.

In order to maximise the length of the load waterline (and this is the one that matters; the designed or datum waterline may, particularly on a very small cruiser, differ by as much as 10 per cent from the actuality), there has been a tendency of late for small yachts (and larger ones too) to do away with any pretence of aesthetics and to extend the waterline length by deftly removing any curve or rake to the stem. This severe approach has also led to the adoption of either a plumb transom stern or one with a reverse rake. Both of these certainly do lengthen the effective waterline (and without adding undesirable weight), but a retroussé stern curtails cockpit space and, at the same time, tends to push the cabin too far forward so that the area on deck is less than would be normal for a given length overall. A recent refinement of the retroussé stern draws the lower edge out beyond the transom itself, thus increasing the waterline length even further. Taken to extremes, though, these 'scoop' sterns are vulnerable to damage and can make the attachment and siting of rudder, backstay and outboard mountings problematical. This said, they do provide an excellent bathing or boarding platform. (And it makes it possible for a salesman, without actually telling an outright lie, to describe a yacht as a 20 footer (and to exact the *price* of a 20 footer) for a boat that is, in effect, some 2 ft (61 cm) shorter!)

Straight stems and plumb transoms are nothing new of course, and many working craft adopted a similar form: the East Coast Bawleys, Solent Smacks, Itchen Ferry and West Country oyster smacks all had overall lengths differing only marginally from that of the waterline. This was also for the same reason – length on the waterline equals speed. (Whether they were actually aware of the formula that determines this – that the square root of the LWL times 1.4 equals speed in knots (where the measurement is given in feet) – is open to argument!)

Quite a few of the cruising yachts built in the 1920s and 1930s followed this well-established pattern, with the uncompromising lines often softened by a suggestion of curvature or rake to bows or transom (and nearly all had a graceful sheerline too). Most opted for a very moderate overhang fore-and-aft, with the waterline length measuring somewhere in the region of 80 per cent of the overall length. Today, a similar proportion is still the norm, and this allows a balance between maximum possible length on the flotation line consistent with a pleasing appearance. The length/waterline length ratio would be quite different for any one of the many classes of day-racing keel boats – and a fair number of these have been quite happily converted into able, if cramped, small cruisers. (However, with the increasing interest in restoration and historical correctness, an equal number seem to be in the process of de-conversion by enthusiasts.) A Pleiad keel boat, with the fine bows and tapering counter stern typical of these traditional designs, has an overall length of 21 ft (6.4 m) and a waterline length of 13 ft (3.9 m) – the waterline being only 62 per cent of the length overall. A similar percentage is also commonplace with the larger keel boats, such as the International Dragon and East Coast One Design, while some of the International Skerry cruisers are even more extreme – with a waterline length not much over half that measured on deck! Elegant though these long overhangs undoubtedly are, they also serve a purpose: that of elongating the effective waterline as soon as the boat heels – and nearly all these slim racing boats heel in anything more than a whisper of breeze. Yet the drawn-out ends, although increasing reserve buoyancy at bows and stern and damping, to some extent, the pitching moment in a head sea, contribute nothing to the accommodation or stowage space; and, at least in wooden yachts, they were (and are) a constant source of structural problems brought about by inadequate ventilation and inaccessibility.

The concept of the micro cruiser is far from new: this pretty 18 ft (5.4 m) Blackwater sloop was constructed just before the Second World War!

Since, arguably, overhangs are nothing more than a costly nuisance, they have – not surprisingly – gone out of fashion, though there are of course exceptions that can be conveniently cited, one of these being the 17 ft (5.1 m) Silhouette Mark II. Without doubt one of the most popular miniature cruisers ever conceived, this craft bears little superficial resemblance to a long-ended flyer but, with a 17 ft (5.1 m) overall length and a waterline of only 13 ft (3.9 m), the proportional figures are very close to those of a racing keel boat!

If there seems to be rather a lot of emphasis here on this factor of waterline length, it is simply because the limitation on hull speed must not be underestimated when planning a passage. And yet, it often is not only underestimated, but totally ignored. It has been said that sailing craft do not have ETAs – only destinations! Brochures might have it otherwise, but there is a kernel of truth in this old maxim – and more than just a kernel in so far as the smallest cruising boats are concerned: after all, a yacht of 14 ft (4.2 m) on the waterline will have a theoretical maximum hull speed of only 5.6 knots. The implication is pretty clear: patience on the part of the crew is going to be a necessity rather than a virtue; for, quite simply, it is going to take a long time to get from A to B. Not that a planing design will necessarily fare much better, even in optimum conditions of flat water and a hustling Force 4 to 5 on the beam. Once weighed down with a full cruising inventory – two anchors, chain, outboard, fuel and water (not to mention human ballast) – it will be lucky to stagger on to the plane! If it does, it will only be by the expedient of hanging on to full sail when common sense would suggest a reef; this will tire the crew early on in the passage, leaving them with insufficient physical resources to cope with severe weather later on.

Coastal waters

Small sailing cruisers are perfectly seaworthy in the right hands – but there is a restricted range of conditions within which the smallest can hope to fulfil anything like full performance potential. This will vary somewhat according to such design attributes as draft, beam, section and windage. Also, the experience and stamina of the crew must be taken into account, as well as the sailing area. In reasonably protected waters, almost any boat can be driven hard in quite heavy weather, and the majority of craft will also be able to make acceptable progress to windward even when reefed. Little is gained by putting this moment off: usually at the upper end of a Force 4 (18 knots or thereabouts), the full mainsail will be partly aback and flogging. Much of the boat's forward drive will be lost; there will be excessive heeling, the natural accompaniment to which is a reduction in draft (which will drastically increase the amount of leeway). In quite a few modern designs, notably those with the maximum beam well aft and transom-hung rudders, the boat will start to luff up uncontrollably as the angle of heel brings the rudder clear of the water.

Downwind, in smooth water, it will be easy to maintain maximum speed, and reefing, though prudent, may not be a matter of urgency since the course is not being constantly deflected by wave action. However, once the hull speed is reached, there is really very little point in clinging on to the full working sail area just for the hell of it – not when cruising, at any rate! Running hard in these conditions, though, can bring another risk entirely: that of failing to realise just how strong the true wind actually is. The apparent wind is effectively reduced by the boat's own speed before it – conversely, it is increased when heading into it! On hardening up to windward there may come a nasty surprise: the craft will at once be overpowered; and this can easily lead to a collision in crowded waters, since an over-canvased boat may not respond to the rudder. Also, the abrupt strain to which spars and rigging are subjected (this is usually exacerbated by violent slatting of the sails) has led to the downfall of quite a few masts.

Sailing in sheltered waters is one thing, but passage making in coastal or offshore seas is another. In this case, there are the added complications of tidal streams, and allowance has to be made for these. The depth of water and the nature of the sea bed must also be borne in mind, since the movement of water that produces waves largely occurs far below the surface. The length of fetch (length of fetch, in simplest terms, refers to the distance over which the wind, unimpeded by land mass, can blow) also directly influences the sea state. All of these things contribute to the size, uniformity of pattern and the steepness of the seas. Recent gales – even those hundreds of miles distant – may also have built up a conflicting swell just to add to the complexity of wave systems! Air temperature too tends to affect the wave size: a chill wind blowing over warmer water often bringing about larger waves than would result when the temperatures are reversed. True, wave height is easy to overestimate, but it is reasonable to suggest that, with a Force 5 wind over tide whipping it up in the Bristol Channel or North Sea, neither yacht nor crew will find things altogether to their liking, whereas in a less exposed river, both might be revelling in it! A wave height of 4–5 ft (1.2–1.5 m) is quite enough for comfort, although much would depend upon the distance between crests and the regularity of the pattern.

The motion of any small sailing vessel can be unsettling, unpredictable or violent – and, not infrequently, a medley of all three! Downwind, all yachts (though the smallest and lightest suffer most) will be alternately slowed and slewed by waves, only to surge forward and accelerate on crests; and not even the most accomplished helmsman can be relied upon to compensate adequately for the yawing engendered by a steep following sea – nor damp out the rolling. If you attempt to pinch right up on the wind in a sharp, short chop, then the resultant pitching can bring a small yacht, quite literally, to a standstill. The only alternative is to bear away, perhaps by as much as 10 degrees, and resign yourself to the inevitability of travelling a greater distance over the ground in order to reach the objective. Unfortunately, the possibility of seasickness affecting one, or even all, of the crew members can never be discounted when adverse weather means the yacht may have to stay at sea for a much longer period than was originally envisaged.

Yet if an excess of wind – especially wind from the wrong direction – is a nuisance, then an insufficiency of the stuff can be quite inconvenient too! Few small cruising boats are at their best in ghosting conditions; and not even specialised light weather ghosters, spinnakers or cruising chutes are nec-

essarily all that much help when at sea, for rarely is the surface of the sea free from surface swell – which causes the boat
to roll slightly and spills any wind from the sails. It is therefore
reasonable to assume that when sailing to windward in
coastal waters or further offshore, satisfactory progress can
only be relied upon in wind speeds of between 8 to 20 knots; if
wind speed is above or below those figures, then a small
craft's performance will suffer noticeably (almost certainly it
will have difficulty in stemming a foul tide that runs at more
than 2 knots). Naturally, certain designs will be more efficient
than others in either light or heavy conditions (few cruising
boats, though, excel at both ends of the spectrum). Those most
affected by extremes are, without doubt, the smallest of the
bilge and triple keelers: this is because of the high drag of
underwater hull and the lack of draft, often coupled with
excessive windage from bulky topsides and superstructure.
Such a hull is frequently matched to a rig with an undersized
sail plan, possibly sails of indifferent cut, and excess windage
due to heavy spars, along with oversized standing and running rigging.

Once off the wind, then matters improve – for a start, it
should at least be feasible to proceed towards the intended
goal in a straight line! Even so, that waterline length/hull
speed ratio still holds true, and an adverse tidal stream will
reduce progress over the ground. Fortunately, tides rarely run
at full strength for more than two to three hours out of six – and
at times will actually act in your favour! Yet working the tides
is of prime importance, and the practice (frequently adopted
by larger vessels) of simply letting contrary tides cancel each
other out over a period of time is definitely not one to be
recommended for a small craft.

This may all seem to suggest that not only is the opportunity
for worthwhile cruising rather limited, but that there is little
prospect either of satisfaction (let alone excitement) when daysailing! However, this is far from the truth: quite ambitious pas-
sages are possible with forethought. And also, because small
boats tend to be highly manoeuvrable and give a sensation of
speed (almost unequalled by larger craft – except possibly in
stripped-out blood and thunder racing machines), sailing in
them can be very exhilarating. On a glorious summer day, 5
knots on a close reach can feel like flying, and memories of
lowering skies and churning seas soon become just that –
memories! To accept the limitations of the boat (and of those on
board) could be regarded by some as adopting a negative
attitude, but 'realistic' would be a more appropriate word.
Once experience has been gained with the boat and crew

attuned to each other, a micro yacht offers some of the most satisfying sailing to be had.

The designer's aims

There are few boats on the market, be they new or second-hand, that are so intrinsically flawed as to be dangerous, although these do undeniably exist. Far more common are examples where dubious construction or design has led to structural problems or behavioural difficulties; and not every one of these will necessarily be the product of an amateur's workshop or drawing board – professionals can (and do) get things wrong! Defects attributable to the builder are usually the result of zealous cost-cutting: economies in quality and quantity of cloth and resin, or scantling sizes whittled to the bone. In the case of a 'rogue' design, there has usually been an over-emphasis on one aspect of performance (or, more commonly, accommodation) at the expense of other attributes.

Experience will help in weeding out those craft with obviously undesirable characteristics, or cursed by distortions brought about by copy-catting IOR rule-cheaters. Most structural faults (if not all) can be unearthed by a competent surveyor (and if defects are overlooked by the surveyor, there is – theoretically at least – some legal redress). The detection of the subtler anomalies originating at the drawing board is not so easy, though. Even skippers with several years' sailing to their credit may be taken by surprise when the new boat turns out to possess a mind of its own – and a hostile one at that! Certain idiosyncrasies cannot be overcome without expensive alterations, and some cannot be overcome at any price; so, as far as design is concerned, a little learning could prove very advantageous to the purchaser – preferably acquired before the cheque-writing ceremony!

No matter what the designer's aim, each sailing boat is subject to laws and of these, the law of compromise is foremost, even though not formally recognised. The effects of this law of compromise are very evident in small craft, where the demands of accommodation have to be reconciled with ease of handling and a reasonable turn of speed under sail. The importance of the latter cannot be too heavily stressed: it is a misconception that a slow boat will be a safe one – indeed, the reverse is true. There is nothing more disheartening than ploughing grimly on in a yacht that cannot attain waterline speed, even in favourable conditions – except perhaps struggling to manoeuvre a badly balanced craft or one that stub-

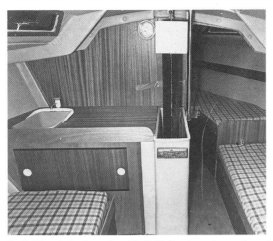

Left *The interior of a 19 ft (5.7 m) cruiser showing the box for the vertical lifting keel. The galley is fitted in around this, and so makes the best use of the available space. A single burner cooker with self-sealing bottle is sited beneath the removable worktop and a fitted plastic bucket makes a very effective sink.*

Normally, a table top would fit over the open keel box – although in any case a lid, with means of retention, should always be fitted when the yacht is on a mooring or under way, since water can slop up into the accommodation. I know of two small boats sunk in this manner during the 1987 gale.

Right *The ingeniously fitted forepart of a 21 ft (6.4 m) junk rigged Coromandel. The mast is well forward, allowing the cooker and swivelling dining table to be sited for ease of use. However, this layout would not be suitable for a boat without a forehatch because of the difficulty of escape if fire breaks out in the galley. (A fire blanket must always be sited in the galley space.)*

bornly refuses to come about in a head sea (and which may, in extremis, have to be worn around, before the wind, in the manner of a square-rigged ship).

Not even professional designers agree upon the various aspects of boat design, and even some basic parameters of performance are now being questioned. However, reducing the subject to the simplest possible terms: the first characteristic, speed under sail, is dependent upon five things. Of these, the first is waterline length, and the second displacement, with lightweights tending to have the upper edge in light to moderate winds. The 'counter agents' are skin friction, water resistance and also the hull's wave-making peculiarities. Now, unfortunately, those attributes that go towards the creation of an able and seaworthy long-distance cruiser (with an easy

Perspectives

These hull perspectives – which are a compound of the waterlines, sections and buttock lines – show the differences between hulls of varying types.

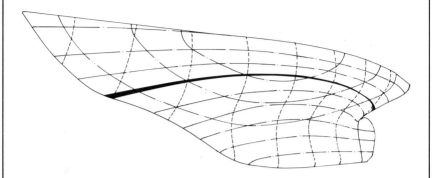

A 'traditional' small cruising boat of the type popular between the wars (and quite in demand today by enthusiasts who can cope with the maintenance of the carvel-built timber hull). Relatively narrow beamed, such boats usually have a long ballast keel faired into a deep forefoot and a gentle turn to the bilge. The bows are fairly fine forward and the topside sections have a degree of flare to keep the boat dry in a chop. A moderate overhang at the bow balanced by a short counter help to give an easy motion in a seaway, as does the good distribution of the ballast. The rudder in this instance is underhung to the after part of the keel, protected from damage but not too efficient in shape (especially when a portion is cut out to accommodate the bearing and propeller of an inboard). Accommodation on an overall length of 22 ft (6.7 m) would not be especially roomy, although since the cabin sole can be taken well down into the turn of the bilge, headroom may be better than might be expected.

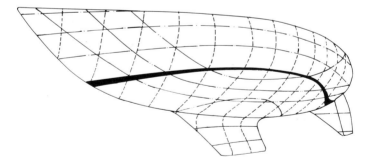

A medium-displacement fin and skeg micro, with canoe body, separate fin keel and an underhung rudder well aft, protected by a skeg. A fairly firm turn to the bilge promises good initial stability, and a degree of tumblehome to the midships topsides sections improves the heeled shape. Reasonable overhangs and a waterline that is virtually symmetrical ensure ease of handling throughout a wide range of wind strengths, although the hull form might be prone to roll downwind. All in all, this is a boat tolerant of a helmsman's mistakes, but rewarding when driven hard. Performance to windward depends greatly upon the draft, and this type of hull may be fin-keeled or fitted with bilge keels or variable draft options.

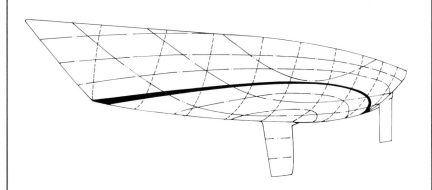

This light-displacement micro has the accent more towards sporty performance, though the high freeboard and a wide beam at deck level allow a surprising amount of room below. However, the resultant windage coupled with a shallow forefoot and the light weight may make it difficult to drive the boat on the wind in heavy weather, especially as the fine waterlines forward, coupled with a broad transom, may result in an indifferent hull balance at a steep angle of heel. The waterline beam is quite narrow and the boat should be sailed as close as possible to upright at all times – which may entail exiling the crew on to the sidedeck! The transom-hung high-aspect rudder gives good control off the wind, but excessive heeling may bring it out of the water – with consequences that can easily be imagined. However, less extreme variants are lively without being too headstrong and will provide excellent sailing within defined limits. The low all-up weight, when allied to the often available option of variable draft in the form of a lift or pivoting keel, makes it possible to trail most behind a medium-sized car.

motion at sea, room for the crew – both on and off-watch – and the capacity to carry sufficient water, stores and emergency equipment) are not usually those that are conducive to speed or an easy motion. This holds true for both sailboats and powerboats (whatever the size), but obviously in a small yacht tolerances are minimal, and there is no room for error: either the boat won't sail or the crew won't fit into the bunks! Ridiculous though this may sound, there have been instances (and given human nature, almost certainly still are) where the designer, mind firmly fixed upon the royalties from a nice long production run, comes up with plans where a subtle (or rather, optimistic) change of scale obscures the fact that the interior of the boat is considerably larger than the exterior!

Accepting that there is no single absolute that will establish the perfect cruising hull form, it is nevertheless possible to look carefully at a yacht and make an intelligent guess as to the designer's intentions, and just how well these are likely to be fulfilled. Of course, this does presuppose at least a theoretical understanding of the way in which a hull is drawn and what effect the sections, the waterlines and the lateral plan have on the yacht. Nowadays, the lines drawings, which are compounded of these three constructs, are not easy to come by (and very rarely available to the buyer of a production boat), but twenty or so years ago they were quite widely published. Valid comparisons can be made from these lines drawings, dated though they may be, and it is easy to understand the way in which the yacht hull evolved from working and trading vessels and to see how designs subsequently diverged into two quite different species. Though there is a degree of overlap, these are, first, the heavy-displacement type with a long ballast keel to which is hung a sharply raked rudder (the so-called classic or traditional cruising vessel), and, secondly, the light and beamy dinghy type of hull with high-aspect, very narrow, fin keel and transom or underhung rudder, both of which are separate entities (or rather, appendages) to the actual hull.

Looking at lines

When looking at a lines drawing, it is immediately apparent that the waterline and lateral plans are divided at regularly spaced intervals: these are known as the stations, at each a section is, in effect, cut straight through the hull. Each of these transverse slices shows the breadth at deck level and waterline, and both of these measurements are critical. Of course, this is not all the information shown: from the midship sections can be deduced the wetted surface area, the stability, and also the displacement (which in turn decides the amount of space below decks).

The narrow waterline beam of a semicircular section has the lowest wetted surface, but is also the least initially stable, so that any gain in light weather performance will be largely offset by lack of sail-carrying power in a blow unless an unrealistic amount of ballast is carried to compensate. This rounded section is also liable to roll murderously downwind and, when coupled with high freeboard and shallow draft (as is frequently the case with small yachts because of the demands of the accommodation), life on board can be singularly nauseous.

Given a midship section of squarer form – that is to say, with a relatively sharp turn to the bilge – there will be greater initial stability, but, for the same displacement, less immersed depth of hull. In other words, there will be minimal headroom within, unless the freeboard is increased (and the law of diminishing returns comes into effect here, ensuring that much of the gain in stability imparted by the underwater section will be cancelled out by the increased windage of the topsides!).

Both of these types of section would, as a rule, be associated with a light-displacement boat; the 'traditional' hull tends to have a midships section more closely approaching that of an inverted triangle, with a soft turn of bilge fairing gently into the keel root. This makes for good headroom in the accommodation, for the cabin sole, though inevitably rather narrow, can be carried well down into the hull. More important, so long as the beam is within average parameters, this midship section, though lacking initial stability (which would be more noticeable with a small yacht than in a larger craft), produces a hull whose stability actually increases with the angle of heel. This ensures that, except in freak conditions, knock-downs are very rare (assuming, of course, that the amount of ballast has been correctly calculated – an average ballast ratio would usually be around 42–50 per cent for a medium- to heavy-displacement cruiser).

The sections of the bow and stern – and the amount of overhang of each – play an important part in determining the motion and, in particular, the degree of pitching to which the vessel is subject in a head sea. The tendency today is to have rather flat, U-shaped sections forward, since these provide buoyancy as long as the boat is sailed upright – and they also help prevent nose-diving under waves when carrying a spinnaker in strong winds! However, these sections can and do slam when driving hard to windward and, when coupled (as they often are) with a shallow forefoot, are inclined to produce a hull form that is easily deflected by wave action. In a flat-sectioned boat with a broad transom though, high downwind speeds can be achieved; and if the displacement is light enough – and the crew determined enough – it should be possible to plane (or at the very least to surf) downwind, if only in small bursts.

Although there were exceptions, notably where boats evolved specifically to deal with local conditions, the working sailing vessels of the last century were inclined to favour rather bluff, full-sectioned bows along with narrowing, slightly Vee'd sections aft. This was not altogether a successful union, since it encouraged 'hobby-horsing' in a head sea; this is a decidedly uncomfortable motion brought about because wave action flings the over-buoyant bows clear of the water and, with insufficient reserve buoyancy in the fine-lined stern sections to counteract and damp this out, the pitching becomes, in effect, self-regenerating.

Narrow Vee sections at the bows slice through waves effortlessly, and therein lies the disadvantage – from the viewpoint

Hull profiles (*not to scale*)

These sketches give an idea how the hull designs of the smallest yachts have evolved in the last fifty years or so – from the heavy-displacement form with long deep keel and a soft section to the bilge (rather reminiscent of a wineglass) to the lighter-displacement types where the hull is shallower (more closely related to a dinghy or canoe) and the keel and rudder are separate appendages.

Since the late 1950s, a good deal of effort has been spent in perfecting shallow and variable draft options for the small yacht, greatly increasing the versatility.

An 18 ft (5.4 m) Blackwater sloop, fairly typical of the smaller cruisers built before and immediately after the Second World War: little apparent concession made to speed (although off the wind such boats were far from sluggish), but a seakindly hull of quite heavy displacement with moderate overhangs, deep forefoot and soft midships sections. This drawing shows a variant with built-up topsides, not common in traditionally constructed craft of this size, since – in spite of an increase in deck area, accommodation space and headroom in the fore cabin – they add undesirable weight forward.

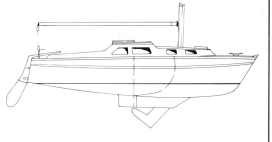

A Kestrel, designed by Francis Jones for one-design racing on the east coast; the boats were first constructed in clinker planking, but later moulded in GRP. Variable draft is achieved by means of an L-shaped steel centreplate contained largely within the ballast keel and bridgedeck. The hull is of shallow section with quite a firm turn to the bilge and short overhangs. Building costs were kept down by the canoe body and separate keel, which are much easier and quicker to construct than a yacht with a garboard tuck.

Brown Trout, a pre-First World War Broads yacht, with very low wetted area and drag – thus very fast, quite manoeuvrable and designed strictly for sheltered waters. Freeboard is very low, the hull sections shallow in the extreme, and keel and rudder are separate appendages. The divided lateral plane, with the underhung elliptical rudder typical of Broads yachts, makes for good directional stability. Accommodation is, by today's standards, a bit restricted (to put it mildly!). Headroom is provided by a lifting canvas coachroof.

A converted 20 ft (6 m) day-racing keel boat, this BBII has a short waterline length in relation to length overall, is narrow, and with almost circular section. To keep costs down, the iron ballast keel is a separate appendage. The conversion (which would upset a purist) manages two berths, two buckets, and

that's about it; such boats are beguiling to sail in reasonable weather and on sheltered waters, but, being lightly built, cannot be regarded as suitable for serious cruising.

The advent of marine plywood made possible some quite adventurous designs, not all of which were regarded at the time as successful from an aesthetic point of view (though many, viewed in retrospect, do seem more attractive). The Debutante had perhaps the most accommodation that could be packed into a 20 ft

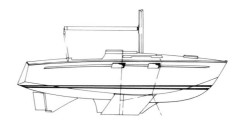

(6 m) hull, and achieved privacy for the occupants by opting for a centre cockpit. The flush decks are practical from the point of view of construction and simplicity, but are less pleasant to work on than might be supposed; without coachroof or cockpit coaming to wedge a foot against when heeled, going forward is more precarious.

The hull, with a single hard chine, can only be described as 'boxy' in section and the original design is woefully under-canvased – so performance is less than sparkling, particularly in light airs. Lateral resistance is provided by the low-aspect twin splayed steel bilge plates, and to a lesser degree by the skeg and rudder; the centreline ballast stub keel provides the righting moment – a configuration that allows the craft to take the ground comfortably and to sail in shallow waters, but could hardly be worse as regards drag and windward efficiency. Also, windage is heavy because of the high topsides.

Hot- and cold-moulded veneer techniques produced some interesting and quite advanced designs, such as the Fairey Atalanta and the Audacity, both of which made full and uncompromising use of the technology and incorporated rolled sidedecks and low-profile coachroofs. The majority of these boats are

still perfectly sound more than thirty years on, but where repairs are necessary, the moulded veneer complicates matters. The example in this sketch has a steel centreplate, like the Kestrel, housed within the ballast keel, very rounded sections with a marked degree of tumblehome in the topsides, and minimal overhangs fore-and-aft.

Performance would be good in light to medium airs, but the slight fullness of the bow coupled with a shallow forefoot are not really an asset when attempting to slice to windward in heavy conditions.

A high proportion of the early small production glassfibre yachts, such as the Snapdragon, Alacrity and Vivacity, used bilge keels, moulded integrally with the hull and containing encapsulated ballast. These were

arguably less efficient to windward, since, without any outward splay, the leeward keel does not approach the vertical (so increasing the draft) once the boat heels. However, the configuration did make it possible to dispense with the centreline ballast stub, so keeping resistance to a minimum. Lack of a skeg on some designs meant they sat on the stern when dried out! Many of these early boats were heavily laid up (enormously so by today's standards), since early glassfibre building principles tended to follow wooden-boat practice – ie the stronger the thicker, and never mind the weight gain!

This 19 ft (5.7 m) lift-keel yacht, the Evolution 19 designed by Julian Everitt, is fairly typical of the modern small yacht: not extreme in form, but with the accent towards performance. Such craft are easily trailed, fast and responsive to handle, and yet somehow manage to

fit in four full-length berths, a galley and a (primitive) toilet!

The hull is of rounded section with a low waterline beam and, in common with the majority of small lightweight boats, is best sailed upright; excessive heeling slows the boat and, because of the broad transom, the rudder tends to lift clear of the water.

Nowadays, there are numerous methods of achieving variable draft, like the E boat and Poacher; the Evolution uses a ballast keel in a trunking that is lifted vertically by a deckhead winch (larger yachts would probably use hydraulic systems to raise the keel). Once the keel is raised, it is housed completely within the hull and the boat is flush bottomed; this is an asset when grounding or trailing, though it does make the fitting of an inboard impracticable because of the vulnerability of the fixed shaft.

Best described as fun with a dash of fashionable styling: many of the latest generation of micros with light hulls and variable draft offer superb sailing in rivers and sheltered coastal waters. In the right hands these boats can be as rewarding to sail as a racing dinghy – with none of the risk of capsize – and make good sporty weekenders, docile enough for the family in moderate conditions. A number of designs have a self-tacking jib and fractional rig with larger mainsail than was the case with a masthead rig; some feature a simplified spinnaker system of an asymmetric reaching spinnaker (a blister) set on a retractable pole.

A modern racing boat, elliptical keel, as narrow as possible at the root to minimise drag and turbulence. The sections are U-shaped and it is important that the boat is sailed upright. Performance in light to medium airs is exceptional, but in heavy weather the boat will need great skill and concentration to sail off the wind, as reaction to the separate rudder will be instantaneous and too much helm movement may bring about a broach. On the wind, the flat section forward means that the hull will pound in waves and be easily stopped by a head sea. Such craft, being generally very lightly built (as well as temperamental in handling), are not well suited for conversion to cruising yachts, although, once outclassed, many are offered for sale at very attractive prices.

of the crew members huddled damply in the cockpit, at any rate! A very wet ride can be guaranteed in a fresh breeze, although a long forward overhang with its reserve of buoyancy may to some extent alleviate this (as well as extending the effective waterline). High freeboard helps keep the cockpit drier too – but at the cost of increased weight and windage.

A finely drawn stern has the obvious drawback of being a poor weight carrier – and this in exactly the area where, in a small boat especially, a high proportion of the sailing weight in the form of the outboard, fuel and human bodies is inevitably concentrated. (It should not be forgotten that four adults whose combined weight might amount to 600 lb (272 kg) would account for around one-fifth of the total sailing weight of certain 20 ft (6 m) yachts – in particular, those aimed at the trail/sailing market!) In the case of a larger boat, an extended counter stern can pay dividends in that it increases the waterline length once the boat is heeled, and provides a reserve of buoyancy that helps to cancel out pitching: arguably, though, this is at too high a cost (both in terms of space and also expense) to justify its existence on a small boat, except on the grounds of aesthetics.

The sections of the topsides have a role in determining whether a boat will be dry or wet in a seaway. It is common for there to be a certain amount of 'flare' or outward curve above the waterline, so that the greatest beam is at deck level; this not only increases the buoyancy of the heeled hull, but softens the slamming effect when pounding into a head sea. It also tends to fling spray clear of the hull and away from the cockpit! (Another way of deflecting the wet stuff is to incorporate a knuckle at the bow, but – though effective – this does little for the heeled shape, and less for the yacht's appearance.)

The opposite to 'flare' is 'tumblehome'; here, the topsides curve noticeably towards the narrowest beam, which is at deck level: this makes for a section comparable to that of a brandy goblet. If carried to excess, tumblehome looks unattractive, but it does improve the heeled shape; it also saves weight, since the deck area is slightly reduced (not entirely a blessing on a small yacht, where the sidedecks are, at best, restricted). It is also a sound design strategy, since it reduces the turbulence at gunwale level; for when the boat heels, the drag from stanchions, lifelines and other miscellaneous deck hardware can be considerable.

Looking once more at the lines drawing, it will be noticed that the hull is divided several times by fore-and-aft cuts parallel to the flotation line; these are the waterlines and they indicate the turn of the bilge as well as the sections at the keel root, topsides and, of course, all intermediate points. The waterlines also show clearly the entry at the bow, and the length and steepness of the run aft. In fact, they either show or clarify each of the curves that, when compounded, produce the hull. Reading the waterlines is rather like interpreting a contour map: the closer the lines appear, the sharper will be the curvature of that part of the hull.

From the waterline plan it can be established at a glance whether the boat is designed on the old axiom of 'Cod's Head and Mackerel's Tail', first laid down as a design principle in the construction of fighting ships in the sixteenth century; or whether the opposite extreme, the so-called 'Wedge of Cheddar' (a fine entry and broad stern), has been adopted. As indicated, the former would be likely to be found in a traditional boat, especially one based on working vessels, but it does have its limitations – perhaps the most notable being a tendency to produce a transverse bow wave of awesome proportions as speed is increased. This is because the water displaced by the passage of the hull is forced upwards (that being the line of least resistance), and, with the bluff bows, outwards as well, thus creating what amounts to a wall of water. Needless to say, this has a detrimental effect on both acceleration and ultimate speed.

Finer waterlines forward produce a hull that tends to slice through water causing a divergent bow wave (or waves) that has little measurable effect on speed. The sections and entry have to be judged to a nicety by the designer: a hull that is too fine in the fore part will bury itself under waves instead of slicing through them, and this propensity will be exaggerated if narrow bows are coupled with too full a stern. (Another compromise is called for here – and one, moreover, that is difficult to resolve in a small yacht, because due allowance must be made for crew weight concentrated in the cockpit.)

No matter what kind of hull form is indicated by the line of the load waterline (and, just occasionally, the load waterline is somewhat at variance with the designed or datum waterline – depending on the accuracy of the designer's calculations), it will, if taken to extremes, result in a boat that becomes ill-balanced, maybe even totally uncontrollable, at a steep angle of heel. This tendency is exacerbated in small boats with buoyant, beamy sterns and transom-hung, vertical rudders, since the blade often comes out of the water when the boat is hard pressed on the wind – the effect on the steering being quite predictable! Ideally, in a cruising boat, the waterlines of bow and stern should be close to symmetrical, and their buoyancies closely matched to one another.

The lateral plan of the hull, vertically divided by 'buttock lines', emphasises the sectional shape and reveals the profile of the underbody – and also that of keel and rudder. This profile provides perhaps the clearest indication of the hull shape; it also highlights the trade-off between out-and-out speed and ease of handling. Basically, the shallower the underbody, the narrower the sections on the waterline, and the flatter the run aft, the faster the craft will be off the wind; but the windward ability depends also upon the boat having sufficient stability to carry working sail up to at least Force 4 without needing to reef – hence the need for adequate ballast, preferably carried on a long lever arm for a greater righting moment. This means a fairly deep keel – which is essential, in any case, to produce the lateral resistance that counteracts leeway. It is the depth of the keel that does most to reduce leeway; the length fore-and-aft is of less relevance – hence the tendency for racing yachts to dispense with as much of the trailing edge as is compatible with the actual attachment of the keel, and to opt for a high-aspect fin, narrow at the root to minimise turbulence at its juncture with the hull. (Yachts designed exclusively for competitive sailing ignore the mundane preoccupations common to those who cruise; drying out alongside a quay or stopping there for a scrub can both be quite hair-raising operations with a short keel!) Unless the rudder is widely separated from the keel and hung to a skeg (which would be anathema in current race boat philosophy), this hull form lacks directional stability; in other words, it over-responds to the lightest touch of the tiller, veers off course at the slightest provocation, and will stubbornly refuse to heave-to.

Quite apart from any structural considerations (narrow fin

keels bolted to ultra-light hulls are prone to damage, to flexing, and sometimes even to sudden and unexpected disappearance), this extreme type of hull form cannot be regarded as viable for a serious cruising boat with all that the term implies. Yet if the limitations are accepted – including the possibility of a fairly short trouble-free life span – such a boat will offer exhilarating daysailing and the possibility of coastal dashes, albeit with a wary eye on the weather.

A hull form with a 'conventional' long keel fairing smoothly into the turn of the bilge presents a large submerged lateral area. This configuration does have the reputation for a certain dignity in the matter of manoeuvring, which is at least partly attributable to the perceived behaviour of extreme examples: there is no doubt that a boat whose length of keel, waterline and on deck are much the same, may not be as quick to respond as one with overhangs and a partially cut-away underbody. An excellent compromise, particularly for a small cruising boat, is that of fairly long (though not full-length) ballast fin keel and a separate aft rudder, underhung to a full deep skeg. This, the divided lateral plan, couples good directional stability with a reduction of lateral area and is noticeably quicker to react. However, both the long-keeled yacht and one of conservative divided lateral type should be capable of self-steer on some points of sailing by the set of the sails alone. It should also be possible without undue difficulty to leave the boat hove-to for long periods. It is by no means unusual for a light boat with narrow fin and cut-away underbody to develop a marked reluctance to tack in a head sea, unless it has good way on, so it may be necessary to bear away slightly before putting the helm up; but, far more unnerving, the boat may come obediently through the eye of the wind only to continue bearing away remorselessly. In so far as the motion in a seaway goes, the 'traditional' hull form is much to be preferred, for the ballast, distributed more evenly along the length of the keel, greatly reduces the tendency to pitch (though this does depend on the balance and harmony of the hull in its entirety).

There is not enough space in this book to give more than the briefest outline of what is commonly held to be a complex and esoteric subject. Yet even a basic grasp of the principles should help a buyer to weigh up hull types, and hence to steer clear of those extremes best avoided.

When all is said and done, the final choice is likely to be determined by the boat's sailing waters and home port: a drying harbour, half-tide mooring or mud berth will rule out a craft with a deep narrow fin; and, although a long-keeled boat *can* take the ground upright supported by beaching legs, there is always an element of risk involved (and, in the case of wooden yachts of clinker or carvel construction, the practice is one to be discouraged since the legs impose considerable stress on the hull, and will over a period of time usually distort the planking and sheerline). Yet even this option, unsatisfactory though it is, is ruled out for fin-keelers, since the minimal keel area renders them unstable; and not even carefully positioned legs can guarantee immunity from tipping on to nose or stern and thence on to one side.

Variable draft options

Although there are heavy-displacement boats whose bilge keels allow them to dry out comfortably, they have often been adapted to do so as an afterthought. Perhaps the ballast keel may be reduced slightly in depth and supplementary bilge runners or keels bolted on. In practice, most of those boats designed specifically to take the ground, whether possessing twin keels or variable draft in the form of a centreplate or lift keel, will have a light- to moderate-displacement hull of fairly shallow form and with a firm turn of bilge (the so-called dinghy type). This is equally true even of older shoal draft cruisers such as the centreplate Dauntless and Sea Kings (beamy clinker-built yachts that can trace their origins back to the tough little Southend beach boats).

The growing popularity of trail/sailing within the last fifteen years or so has resulted in a range of ways to achieve shallow draft without any compromise of seaworthiness, strength or the ability to self-right from a knock-down. The advent of glass-fibre construction has played a large part in this by making it possible to design centreplate and lift keel cases that, moulded integrally into the hull structure, are robust and – unlike their timber counterparts – remain free from leaks! Usually, it is possible to incorporate the case or trunking wholly or partly within the internal accommodation modules, thus eliminating another big drawback: restriction of the sole area and thus available living space. With GRP, it is also easy to encapsulate lead or iron ballast in resin beneath the cabin sole; this is a vast improvement upon the old system of loose ingots or pigs which, unless cast to fit into specific sections of the bilge, were all but impossible to secure against a knock-down, could physically damage a wooden hull, and required annual cleaning. Internal water ballast tanks – quickly drained ashore so as to remove up to one-fifth of the vessel's dead weight for towing –

or winching on to the trailer) – have proved a simple and cost-effective form of ballast for the smaller yacht. These, as with encapsulated metal, can be used in conjunction with either single- or twin-lifting keels, boards or plates designed to operate through the ballasted area of the bilge and so avoid any obstruction into the actual accommodation.

The type and construction of centreboard or plate varies according to the purpose, ie whether it is designed to increase the righting moment or merely to prevent leeway. Often, when used in conjunction with internal ballast, the board (or bilge boards) will have just enough negative buoyancy to ensure immersion when lowered. This means that it can easily be raised without assistance from a winch – clearly an advantage (especially if grounding inadvertently!). However, with the entire weight of ballast contained entirely within the hull, the centre of gravity will inevitably be quite high; consequently, the hull *shape* must have sufficient stability and buoyancy to withstand a knock-down – remember that the board or boards will provide lateral resistance and lateral resistance only. A ballasted plate or keel(s) that has a proportion (even though necessarily a small proportion) of its total weight on the end of a lever arm must be regarded as a better bet for a cruising boat, and it does allow the hull to be designed with rather less beam and reduced windage in the topsides.

The design of lifting and pivoting ballast keels has been refined to the point where arguably one or other type can claim to be the perfect compromise; for a trail/sailer this claim is justified, since the keel can retract completely – leaving a flush-bottomed hull that requires only inches of water for launch or recovery. There will of course be a case or trunking that will obstruct the cabin to some extent, though a bit of ingenuity will usually make it possible to fit the saloon table or part of the galley units around it. With a weight of between (approximately) one-third to two-fifths of the vessel's all-up weight – say 800 lb (363 kg) for a 20 ft (6 m) trail/sailer – the keel will rely upon a winch or hydraulic system to raise and lower it, and the type and siting of this will depend upon the keel: in boats where it lifts vertically, the purchase may be mounted on the deckhead above the keel and taken to a convenient strong point. Often the winch and tackle are demountable (though experience has proved to me that removing the whole set-up and consigning it to a locker is a cast-iron guarantee of running aground – and on a falling spring tide!). Although there have been one or two designs where the lifting keel, once lowered, was left to its own devices – in other words, remained (with luck) in the lowered position, suspended merely by weight and the controlling wires – common sense dictates that locking bolts be fitted, and to sail without these is asking for trouble. Once fitted, the type of locking system used on the E boat – where twin bolts screw down into heavy cross bars – is claimed to allow the boat to dry out alongside a quay standing on the lowered keel, as with a fixed fin. (From a structural viewpoint, there seems no reason to doubt this, but in fact the keel is very narrow and great care would have to be employed in such an operation.)

As the expression implies, a lifting keel is raised vertically (as is a daggerboard) and a swing keel pivots horizontally in the manner of a centreboard; one of the arguments against the former is that if the boat is unfortunate enough to strike a submerged obstruction or run hard aground, there is a greater chance of damage to the keel (and probably also the trunking) than if the keel can swing aft, however slightly, about its pivot bolt, and so partially absorb the force of the impact. In practice, both horizontally and vertically lifting keels should be looked upon as permanent appendages and treated as such once lowered: as with a fixed fin, any force severe enough to move or wring the keel would probably also cause serious trauma to the hull itself. However, it could well be a different story in the case of a centreplate, since this is rarely locked down and would almost certainly avoid serious damage by the ability to pivot. A board or plate that lifts in the vertical plane is quite vulnerable to injury, and for this reason they are quite rare – particularly in monohulls.

Other methods of keeping draft to a minimum include a vertically lifting keel (or twin bilge keels) where the major portion of the ballast is carried in a bulb at the lower edge, or has – in accordance with modern trends – wings or 'winglets' incorporated into the ballast: the idea being to increase 'lift' slightly and also to increase the heeled draft. Both of these variants are efficient, since the righting ballast is sited as low as possible in order to maximise leverage. Another option is to combine a centreplate with an external ballast stub: the plate is housed entirely within the keel, thus eliminating the need for an internal casing. Structurally it is also sound practice, both in timber and GRP boats, and routine maintenance of plate and pivot bolt is simplified by the easy access.

Bilge keels

Given that the most efficient underbody form in terms of speed and aggressive performance on the wind is that of a shallow hull form, with a separate deep narrow fin, all variable and shallow draft boats have to accept a degree of compromise – good lateral resistance against an intrusive trunking and the need for some form of lifting mechanism with its attendant complications.

Fixed twin bilge keels, though with a relatively high drag, are sturdy enough to withstand the stresses imposed by taking the ground twice a day on an exposed half-tide mooring – and doing this for months at a time. Thus, for many owners, this last option is preferable; the simplicity and strength of a bilge-keel configuration far outweighs the slight loss of pointing ability (which in a cruiser might be reckoned to be more than compensated by a noticeable diminution in rolling on a dead run).

The design of bilge keels has come a long way since they were first made popular in the 'pocket cruisers' of the 1960s: these, the forerunners of modern micro yachts, were designed to be built (often by amateurs) from marine plywood (occasionally moulded veneer), but were later adapted for glassfibre. It was these small yet able cruisers – a high percentage of them from the drawing board of the late Robert Tucker – that really brought ownership of a sailing boat within the reach of the average person; not only were they inexpensive to buy or build, but the shoal draft and ability to take the ground upright meant they could be moored in those creeks and tidal estuaries ruled out for the pre-war deep-draft yachts. Although there is a tendency to think of these little cruisers collectively as bilge-keeled, many were in fact triple keelers with the righting ballast carried in a centreline stub keel of cast iron; lateral resistance (such as it was) was imparted by shallow twin keels, usually with a slight outward splay. Fabricated from steel plate and through-bolted via a flange to internal stringers, these proved rugged enough to withstand grounding, but could be repaired (or replaced) simply in the event of damage or corrosion. Hydrodynamically speaking, they left a lot to be desired, and the drag of the four appendages (for the majority also boasted a separate skeg and rudder) was disproportionate to their size; fortunately, these vessels sailed on gamely, unaware of this. Many are sailing still, some 35 years later!

As GRP construction took over from production building in timber (and boatowners in general grew more knowledgeable), so more effort was applied to refining the design of both hull and keels. Initially, glassfibre technology followed the practices involved in the construction of timber craft: basically, to increase strength, increase both size and thickness! Many of these early GRP boats are massive in comparison with today's; performance might have been sacrificed, but, structurally,

The majority of small yachts can be easily trailed and – using a breakback trailer – can be launched without even getting wet feet!

most of these craft have remained sound apart from localised stress crazing around deck fittings, and the inevitable 'battle scars'!

At first, bilge plates or ballasted keels were bolted directly to internal stiffeners, even though there was often a token attempt made to fair the keel root into the underbody. Before very long, though, the possibility of moulding bilge keels integrally with the hull and encapsulating the ballast inside these occurred to manufacturers (in quite a few of these early production boats, the manufacturers were the designers too – especially of any 'stretched' Mark II versions!).

Straightforward though the bilge keel configuration appears initially, the trade-off between strength, windward ability and practicality requires careful thought: in order to point reasonably high, the keels need to be as deep as possible; however, the *'raisons d'étre'* of a bilge-keeler are shallow draft and the ability to take the ground. Ideally, the keels should be as slim as possible and of hydrofoil section to minimise water resistance, but this is harder than it sounds since most, if not all, of the righting ballast is concentrated in them. Integrally moulded GRP keels, though free from the irritating structural problem that may beset those of the ballasted 'bolt-on' variety (ie loosening of the keel studs or bolts due to constant grounding on compacted sand or mud), are of necessity thicker in section than cast-iron keels of the same weight. This is due to the nature of the ballast within the keel: usually a mix of resin and metal pellets or punchings (but the substitution of more economical forms of metal scrap has been rumoured to occur from time to time!), and has less weight per cubic inch than cast iron. The GRP skin on inner and outer edges of the keels adds another 1/2 in (1.2 cm) as well: it all adds up.

Unfortunately, siting ballast of any sailing boat in two keels, either side of the centreline, is not entirely logical; the reason for this is fairly obvious: the minute the boat heels, the windward keel is doing its best to exert a righting moment, but is at the same time battling to counteract the effort of the leeward keel – which is busy immersing the hull ever deeper in the water! This is a basic fact of life so far as bilge-keeled boats are concerned, and one that must be accepted – although the effects can be mitigated by angling the keels outwards from the roots (though this increases the likelihood of movement of the through-fastenings if the boat grounds regularly). This splay, usually between 10 and 15 degrees, also helps to increase the lateral resistance of the heeled hull because the immersed keel, biting deeper into the water, approaches the optimum vertical angle – increasing the draft as the angle of heel intensifies. Meanwhile, the weather keel adopts an attitude closer to the horizontal, so maximising the righting leverage.

Accepting that there are always limitations with twin keels, there is no doubt that splay helps performance on the wind, but it is difficult to mould such keels integrally with the hull and so encapsulate the ballast. It can be done, but it requires a split mould – and this increases tooling costs. There are instances where the boat is designed for the option of either a centreline fin or twin keels; once ballasted, these are laminated into place after the basic hull lay-up is completed. While there is nothing intrinsically wrong with the system, all too often poor attention to fairing and filling leaves visible 'flash marks' that mar the appearance of the underbody.

Triple keels really have little going for them except for the location of the righting ballast, the major part being positioned (usually) in the central keel where it is most effective. Yet the drag of three keels, and possibly also of a separate skeg, is detrimental to performance; and this will be particularly noticeable in the small cruiser because of the unavoidable high ratio of appendage to underbody surface. When it comes to taking the ground, it might seem that 'two legs good, three legs better' would prove to be the case, but a triple keeler cannot safely be left to its own devices on a drying mooring with an uneven surface: there is the risk that the boat will ground on middle and outer keel only and tilt over. Tipping on to the nose or, if the boat does not have a skeg, the stern, is quite common with both triple- and bilge-keeled boats – certain designs are notorious for it! A bit of extra weight (perhaps in the form of water containers) placed at the opposite end can help, although often all that can be done if the boat settles by the stern, is to lift or retract the blade of the rudder or remove it altogether. In a wooden boat, the lower transom edge will be susceptible to damage or erosion of the planking, so it might be wise to fit a protective capping strip to this. And, if staying on board, don't forget that the boat suffers from this problem of stability in the fore-and-aft plane – failure to take appropriate compensatory action could lead to a rude awakening in the night!

The right rudder

Rudders really merit a chapter of their own; they are arguably the single most important fitting, yet most are prone not only to physical damage, but to structural breakdown as a result of poor design. To have a rudder carry away at sea is quite bad enough – though given time and searoom, it is not difficult to cobble together a jury steering system, especially if some fore-thought has been given to this in advance (as it should have been!). However, to lose the rudder unexpectedly in confined waters could result in a collision with a commercial vessel or high-speed power craft, and this is potentially far more serious.

The majority of multi-keelers employ a fixed low-aspect rudder, underhung via a stock and heel bearing to a full skeg; the skeg not only improves the water flow to the rudder, but provides a secure attachment point for the lower bearing and protects the blade itself. Such a unit has the advantage of withstanding the varying stresses encountered both under sail and when taking the ground. However, since it is not practical to have the blade deeper than the keels themselves, this has to rely for much of its surface area in the width rather than depth. This means that a greater angle of helm is required in manoeuvring, and this can slow the boat down. With transom-hung rudders, though those of most bilge-keelers are fixed, there are designs that have opted instead for horizontally lifting blades – and a number of owners have chosen to make such a modification to previously fixed rudders.

This leads to one important point worth noting in yachts with variable draft: the rudder should lift or pivot in the same plane as the keel; there is little point in having a centreplate able to pivot freely in the event of impact, only to expose fixed or vertically lifting rudders to damage. In a way it is a pity that since rudders lifting in the vertical plane, within a fixed head, have a far more positive 'feel' even when partly raised, there has been a tendency to favour them regardless of the format of the lift keel or plate, this in spite of higher risk of injury. While this type of collision might do no more than scratch the painted surface of a keel, it could knock the hell out of an unprotected rudder and, in all likelihood, damage gudgeons and pintles. With glassfibre yachts, any repair work is liable to be complicated by a need to cut away a portion of the cockpit moulding in order to reach the hangings in question; regrettably, this problem of inaccessibility is a common one, and it can mean that attention to keelbolts, deck fittings, etc can be time-consuming, and far more costly than would otherwise be the case.

Making a comparison between differing forms of fixed rudders is hard to do with any real degree of accuracy: designers have their own pet theories and stick to them – often, it seems, flying in the face of common sense as time and again, certain rudders – and those constructed of foam-cored glassfibre in particular – suffer from stress damage and/or delamination. The main reason for the troubles associated with GRP are due (as indeed are nearly all structural evils in whatever material) to moisture permeation. This usually occurs either at the heel bearing or at the upper edge of the blade where the stock is encapsulated (another prime site is the external through-fastenings of pintles). Flexing of the blade, slight though this may be, tends to hasten this process by instigating movement in any internal component. Once moisture has seeped in, two things happen: first of all, the metal stock corrodes, and even the slightest corrosion allows more water to penetrate, thus saturating the core of the blade. Then the foam expands and forces the laminated sections apart, and as a consequence of this, the cycle of deterioration is speeded up by the ingress of yet more water!

So far as strength is concerned, there is much to recommend the good solid old-fashioned 'barn door' – a rudder hung to the trailing edge of a long deep keel – hung with heavy strapped pintles and a substantial heel bearing. This will withstand a good deal of neglect, and is far less likely to be damaged by impact or grounding than any other kind. Nowadays, nearly all small cruisers if not fitted with a transom-hung rudder, are designed with an underhung blade, usually to a skeg and separated from the ballast fin or fins; so long as the skeg is as deep as the rudder itself and of adequate lay-up (many are not), this is fine. However, a number of boats

Emergency steering

Though a soundly constructed rudder should never fail, it does nevertheless happen from time to time. The reasons vary, but minor damage sustained by grounding might have gone unnoticed, fittings corrode and fibreglass rudders in particular are subject to two insidious problems caused by water penetration: delamination of the blade, or unsuspected weakening and eventual breakdown of the internally bonded metal stock. The moral is of course to inspect the boat ashore prior to the start of each season – and always after an accidental grounding!

If the steering is lost in unrestricted offshore waters, there is time to sort things out at leisure – even though the immediate reaction may be one of panic! On a crowded river or anchorage, the consequences may be more serious, if not life-threatening. Collision with another craft can prove both embarrassing and expensive. Though perhaps not in the best nautical tradition, freeing off all sheets and chucking a bucket over the quarter (preferably a galvanised item which will sink at once and whose handle will not immediately tear itself free!) will cause a small boat to lose way and minimise the risk of an incident for the moments needed to improvise some sort of paddle (though a sweep is a valuable item of any yacht's inventory). Accepting that a congested river may not be the appropriate place to experiment, it is possible to steer with a bucket or drogue towed over the stern – worth practising before an incident occurs.

At sea there will probably be sufficient time to adjust sails and steer by rig alone – though a small boat is quickly deflected from its intended course by wave action and would need constant attention. If there is wind vane self-steering gear with a servo rudder, there is no problem, the boat can be steered solely by this, although the sail area may need to be reduced and the balance of the rig must be near perfect. Any yachtsman should really give some prior thought to emergency steering and some basic ideas are sketched out here.

First of all, get way on the boat if necessary. Some boats are so well balanced that they will sail on regardless. However, a rudder which is damaged – possibly wrenched or jammed – as opposed to one which has completely sheared, will cause wildly unpredictable behaviour which could be dangerous in the vicinity of other craft.

A partly submerged bucket will bring a small cruiser up short and at least allow the crew a breathing space and time to size up the situation.

In the case of a boat with a transom stern, hinged steps, obtainable in most chandlers, can be adapted and reinforced to serve as emergency rudder hangings. For the jury rudder, simply ensure that one section of cabin or cockpit sole is of adequate length and thickness; a basic tiller can be slotted over the head or bolted to it.

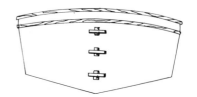

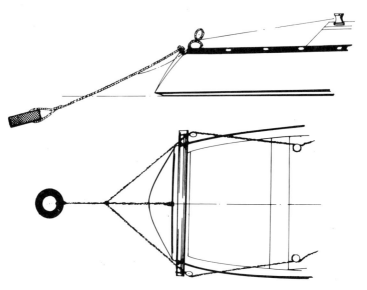

A tyre, drogue or bundle of fenders lashed together can be towed astern and will give more effective control than a bucket. If attached to a pivoting beam, control lines can be rigged and the boat steered from the cockpit.

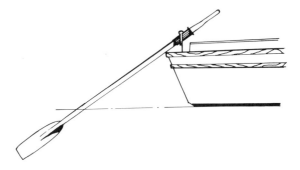

A long scull or sweep is easy to use and every yacht should really carry one, but if there is an aft coaming, an extended oar crutch may be needed to operate the sweep effectively.

A mechanical wind vane self-steering gear, with vertically acting servo rudder, will steer the boat even if the main rudder is lost or damaged. It may be necessary to reduce the sail area. Certainly, careful adjustment of sails will be essential to ensure the near perfect balance of the rig.

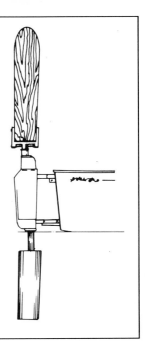

– including, surprisingly, those designed for a drying mooring – have a vestigial skeg, or one that only extends to half – possibly three-quarters – of the draft of the blade; this is barely sufficient even to justify the claim of improved water flow and offers no protection whatsoever when grounding or from possible impact. Not surprisingly, cracking of the laminate is far from unusual – the first signs usually consisting of hairline crazes radiating across the blade aft from the bottom bearing of the skeg. Cracking of the underside of the blade is also common, but in the early stages structural damage is often obscured by a heavy build-up of antifouling – so a meticulous examination of the rudder should be a high priority when it comes to the annual maintenance programme; lack of regular inspection is probably one of the biggest contributory factors to the breakdown of the steering. All pintles, gudgeons and straps must be checked over, especially in modern small craft where these fittings are often fabricated on the basis that lightness is more important than strength – more economical too, though few manufacturers will admit it!

Ballast and buoyancy

Except in the few instances where lateral resistance and stability are obtained directly from hull form (there are relatively few – even Thames barges and the beamy, flat-sectioned traditional working vessels of Dutch waters rely on leeboards for lateral resistance and the payload, be it fish or cargo, for at least part of their stability), it is the yacht's ballast keel (or keels) that allows it to make headway against the wind, to stand up to the sail area, and to recover from a knock-down. However, if the worst should occur – the vessel be holed, the hatches carried away, or the boat suffer failure of a skin fitting, or broach, or perhaps even invert completely due to a rogue wave (in short, if anything leads to a rapid and uncontrollable ingress of water) – it is that ballast keel, or rather the ballast carried by the keel, that could well ensure the boat's demise (a fact that those biased towards multihulls will never lose an opportunity to point out!).

This 'negative buoyancy' element of yacht design has not escaped the notice of designers and those whose preoccupation is with drawing up (and, in the near future, enforcing) standards of construction and equipment for small boats: new craft will be required to be not only self-righting, but also unsinkable. This latter attribute, to put it mildly, is not easy to achieve, thanks to the high proportion of ballast in any sailing boat, although one proposed partial solution (from the United States) is as follows: if swamped and in imminent danger of sinking, simply jettison the keel! Since a major preoccupation for the majority of those who sail is that the keel remain fixed firmly in place, this idea might not be greeted with unrestrained enthusiasm – though it is not really as idiotic as it sounds at first hearing. The arguments for and against the jettisonable keel are fierce, and the opposing factions hurl contradictory figures and formulae at each other with great animation. One drawback is that of constructing a system that could be manipulated at a time of crisis; in the dark with water rising fast, there might only be two or three minutes in which to operate the retaining mechanism. Undoubtedly, a simple and effective locking device could be manufactured, but the engineering would have to be precise – and such precision is expensive.

The stability of the unballasted (and partially swamped) hull would also be very dubious, even if all weights were calculated correctly and sufficient positive buoyancy built in (and if the owner has refrained subsequently from burdening the hapless yacht with excess heavy metal in the form of an oversized stove, spare outboard, additional ground tackle, etc). It is argued that without the ballast keel it should be possible to sail the waterlogged boat safely downwind, given favourable weather conditions (no way could it hope to make up to windward). Yet, without that keel, the centre of gravity will be very much higher, and although the static stability might still be

An interesting little boat and great fun to sail, the 15 ft (4.5 m) Rainbow is una-rigged with an unstayed mast that flexes to spill wind. Although the appearance is perhaps closer to that of a large dinghy, there are two berths and room for a camping stove below the foredeck. Expanded foam under the soles makes it unsinkable.

enough to prevent an immediate capsize caused by rolling in a moderate swell, the wave pattern likely to be encountered during a gale (or as the aftermath) could well overcome any residual inclination to self-right. Unfortunately, too, it is a fact that most beamy yachts with low coachroofs would, without the righting ballast in place, be more stable when inverted – as is the case with multihulls. Once the hull is upside-down, the mast and sails with their associated weight and drag would have the same effect as a keel, and hence effectively ensure the continued inversion.

If the boat remained upright – though bereft of its keel – and a serious attempt were made to sail, wave action would unquestionably induce a pendulum roll – with the momentum increasing until the inevitable outcome could only be a capsize, followed by complete inversion. The consequences for the crew below can be imagined all too vividly: if all deck and cockpit hatches and windows are not absolutely watertight, the boat would fill and, even though prevented from foundering by integral buoyancy, those on board might find themselves trapped. This scenario could only be avoided by the provision of a heavy-duty submersible escape hatch on the underside of the hull – a ploy that is increasingly adopted by larger multihulls.

As has been pointed out, incorporating sufficient buoyancy to keep a ballasted hull afloat when swamped requires comprehensive calculations; after all, every boat has in its construction and inventory items of positive buoyancy: timber, and/or foam-cored GRP, berth cushions and partially filled water or fuel tanks; of neutral buoyancy: food and sails; and with negative buoyancy: engine, all metal fittings (and fastenings) and the keel. Built-in buoyancy will inevitably cut down on accommodation and storage space; this will be particularly noticeable on the small yacht, but it can be done. In fact, it has been successfully achieved by a number of production builders in the United States, Britain and the Continent. With a new GRP boat, it is normal practice to use a partially double-skinned hull moulding with urethane foam 'blown' into the cavities – though, as there are now misgivings as to the use of CFCs in this process, new products and application methods are under review. From a practical aspect, more questionable is the tendency to absorb water by many of these foams and, should the boat in question be holed, moisture will seep through the encapsulated foam – and lead, sooner or later, to serious problems with the laminate.

Wooden boats pose a different set of problems when it comes to the provision of reserve buoyancy. While it is perfectly feasible to fill cavities or compartments of a plywood or moulded boat with foam so long as the internal surface of the timber is completely sealed by resin, obviously this is impractical with clinker or carvel construction. There are several reasons for this: the first being the impossibility of ensuring a waterproof seal between timbers, thus allowing damp, the precursor of rot, to collect behind the urethane. The second is that both planking and frames must be able to flex, albeit slightly, and the foam could prevent this. The foam also expands as it sets, and if the quantity is not accurately judged, then there is a real risk that it will force timbers apart as it hardens – and also a very strong chance that foam droplets will insinuate into joints, separating these. Attempting to foam-fill sections of a boat of whatever construction after it has been built is a certain recipe for later problems; there is no way of ensuring a sound bond with the hull, and if voids are left – as they are sure to be – the way is clear for condensation to form, with wet rot or osmotic blistering (and possible delamination) following hard on its heels.

The yacht – safest liferaft

In recent years, there has been an increased public awareness of the number of fatalities that appear to have occurred as a direct result of the crew abandoning a stricken yacht far too hastily after deciding that their best chance of survival lay instead with the liferaft. Sadly, this faith has very often proved to be misplaced: there are numerous documented instances where liferaft and occupants have been lost without trace, while the yacht was later discovered drifting, often unscathed. Perhaps surprisingly, the surviving vessel has often been a conventional ballasted keel boat, and one without any form of positive buoyancy. This being so, it makes it all the stranger that this tragedy is re-enacted time and again; though, hopefully, if the crew are assured that their boat does have sufficient positive buoyancy to keep it afloat no matter what, they will have confidence enough to remain on board. Of course, for those who have never experienced an emergency at sea – or even a protracted gale offshore – it is easy to point out the foolishness of merely exchanging one dubious risk for another. Yet only someone who has had first-hand experience of enduring bad weather in a small yacht, confined perhaps for days in a cramped space, uncertain of the outcome and feeling powerless to influence it in any way, can really claim to understand the mental stress involved. The incessant noise, the exhausting motion of the boat – to say nothing of fear – can mislead the crew into the belief that any change of circumstances and surroundings can only be for the better. The brain is so numbed that rational decision-making goes by the board, and the consequences of abandoning ship – irrevocable as this decision almost invariably is – cease to be of any concern. Escape is all.

Logically, there seems no reason to take a chance on exposure and possible shortage of food in a liferaft fabricated from inflated rubber or Hypalon tubes when these identical tubes can keep the yacht itself afloat, and here they also benefit from the additional protection afforded by the yacht's own hull! Admittedly, this proposition is hardly new or in any way radical; after all, racing dinghies have long relied upon air bags for flotation after a capsize and, 30 years ago, it was suggested that all small cruisers should carry with them a child's inflatable dinghy or paddling pool. (The inflatable dinghy we know today was then in its infancy, and too expensive to be attained by the majority.) This lightweight plastic boatlet, or whatever, could – if need arose – be inflated in the cabin space and would at least buy time! One or two skippers, intent on one-upmanship, purchased surplus armed forces liferafts with CO_2

inflation – unreliable though this was after several years' storage! These rafts were otherwise usually in a reasonable state and came complete with fish-hooks and line, a floating knife and paddles of a sort, but they did need very careful checking over prior to use – I remember that the one I bought had everything included in the valise except for the all-important plug! Still, for about £30 in today's money, what could you expect? Nowadays, flotation bags for a 20 ft (6 m) boat would cost at least ten times that amount, and more where emergency CO_2 inflation is specified. The modern product, though, would be vastly superior; for a start, each unit would be specifically designed and constructed to keep a waterlogged (and possibly quite extensively damaged) boat afloat, and for a long period of time too – always assuming that the basic arithmetical calculations are correct (these are simple enough in the case of a small yacht); and that proper provision has been made for adequate means of securing the bags, since these, once inflated in earnest, place a very considerable strain upon the vessel's structure. Simply stuffing the buoyancy under berths and into cockpit lockers and then hoping against hope that the flimsy plywood ceilings or shock-cord will retain everything in situ once under load is over-optimistic; the bags will simply tear loose. Eyebolts must be specially fitted to strong points within the hull – one answer would be to reeve attachment lines through the limber holes in frames or floors.

What might be overlooked is the need to protect the bags from chafe once in use – not only from any projecting screws or fittings, but also from contact with the hull or deckhead itself. Some form of protection between the flotation bag and anything with which it comes into contact should be provided – perhaps carpet or foam rubber strips. The distribution of the buoyancy also matters; the hull must be as stable as possible in the lateral and fore-and-aft planes when swamped. The recommended practice is to stow the bags as low as possible, the theory being that the boat will then float higher in the water; in practice, though, if the ingress of water continues in spite of all attempts to pump or bail, the boat will fill. If this should happen, the hull will be more stable with the buoyancy high, under the decks.

Effective as air bags can be in use, they require inspection and maintenance on a regular basis.

Obviously, the provision of buoyancy must be regarded as an important step towards safety at sea, but there are many minor modifications that make the small yacht more efficient and easier to sail; even increased crew comfort, both on- and off-watch, can contribute towards increased security.

2 Deck, Cockpit and Hatches

It has to be accepted that there is little an owner can do about the basic design of the hull, or for that matter the decks or coachroof, but it is possible to make certain alterations to the cockpit layout and to that of the accommodation. The same holds true of the sail controls and deck fittings – indeed, the deck fittings of many small boats purported to be suitable for cruising are thoughtlessly sited, lamentably undersized and poorly attached. Companion and cockpit hatches also fall victim to a boatyard's 'economy drive' and often tend to be flimsy in the extreme, while forehatches on small boats are all too often conspicuous by their absence.

There is much emphasis placed upon the desirability of all sail handling being carried out from the cockpit without the need for any foredeck work at all, and this goes a long way to explain just why it is that so little thought is given to either the design of the deck and its non-slip properties. True, so far as actual area is concerned, the small boat is limited by the demand for sitting headroom below; this can usually be obtained under the coachroof rather than the sidedeck, so width must be sacrificed. In many boats, in particular the smallest of the GRP craft, the coachroof is carried well forward and fairs into what can best be described as a vestigial foredeck: one that is both cambered and sloping, and so can be quite treacherous – particularly when it is heeled at 20 degrees and heaving up and down. Coachroofs tend to be heavily cambered, because of the demand for headroom below, and coamings sharply inclined inwards (aesthetics and windage allegedly to blame here) and this further restricts the area. Should the main hatch consist of either an acrylic panel or lightweight GRP moulding (both types are commonplace), it will hardly be rigid enough for an adult to step upon it with confidence – and this limits room to manoeuvre! And make no mistake, there will be occasions when moving around on deck or coachroof will be unavoidable – halyards, reefing lines and sheets all tangle and jam in spite of the best efforts of human endeavour.

The determination to avoid going on deck at any cost seems to be rather self-defeating – after all, it is part of the physical

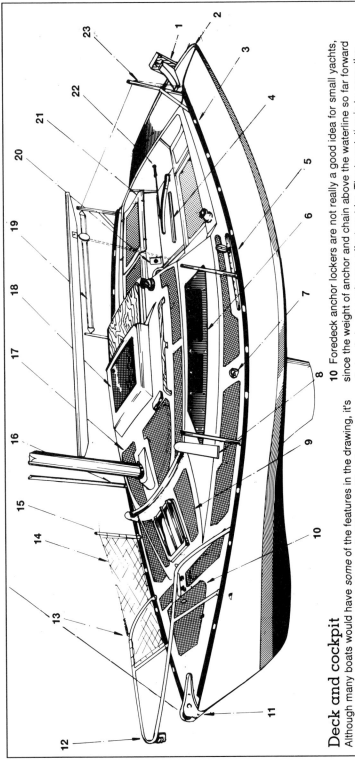

Deck and cockpit

Although many boats would have *some* of the features in the drawing, it's very doubtful if any one craft would have *all* of them – either the good or the bad!

1 The outboard bracket must be sited so that the outboard is within easy reach for starting, raising or lowering – or bringing back on board.

10 Foredeck anchor lockers are not really a good idea for small yachts, since the weight of anchor and chain above the waterline so far forward obviously has an adverse effect on trim. The temptation is to carry the smallest anchor possible and use chain instead of warp; a cruising boat *must* have adequate ground tackle.

11 A good stemhead fitting with roller for chain is essential on any cruising boat.

2 A cut-away or scoop stern makes a fine swimming platform, but does not make boarding from a dinghy any easier. In heavy weather it is essential that the stern can be sealed with a washboard. (Remember, even in lighter conditions, sheets have a tendency to be washed through and may tangle with the prop. Other loose gear (or even small children) also need watching, so it is best to rig a safety net at all times.

3 Aluminium toe rails serve a multiple purpose: joining the hull and deck moulding, providing an anchorage for feet, and also for the siting of temporary lead blocks for spinnaker, vangs, etc.

4 With a wide cockpit sole, it may be difficult for the crew to wedge their feet securely when the boat heels; a timber or alloy brace may be worth fitting.

5 Adjustable sheet leads are essential, and some degree of alteration to the angle of attack on a beamy boat may also be desirable.

6 Overlaid acrylic windows can be very strong, as long as the actual aperture is not oversized. Keep a check on the state of the panels, and if crazes develop on the fastenings (which should be through-bolted, not screwed), replace the window. Check sealant regularly, and also the surrounding area of coachroof for stress crazing.

7 The deck surrounding the shroud eye plates should be carefully watched for signs of crazing. The eyes must always be taken down to a strong point on the hull in order to distribute the loading of the rig. Sometimes, however, they are not, and if the boat is lined internally, this cannot be immediately ascertained. Though common, the practice of carrying cap and lower shrouds to a single bolt is not ideal; if the eye fails – and they can do – the mast will certainly carry away.

8 Many small yachts now fit self-tacking headsails: check the track is mounted so as not to snag oilskins (or light-weather sails). It must be strong enough to use as a hand or foothold.

9 Non-slip panels are essential on the sloping foreside of a coachroof, and also on flush-fitting forehatches.

12 Not even the most powerful bi-colour navigation lights will be visible at sea if mounted as low down as this; use them for a back-up, but if planning on night sailing, try to carry a masthead tri-colour.

13 Sails easily slip through the guardwires, so it is a good idea to use netting forward.

14 It should be possible to free off guardwires to bring back on board a crew member who has gone over the side. It also helps if they can be eased when boarding from a dinghy (or when the boat is craned), as these strains will damage the area surrounding each stanchion base. There must be lanyards at one end and that can be cut through instantly, and perhaps a pelican hook at the other.

15 Stanchions may actually be a nuisance on a small yacht with narrow sidedecks as they restrict movement and can also snag oilskins. Arguably, it is better to develop self-confidence and a sense of balance.

16 Shroud rollers do protect the sails, but if revolving freely they turn the shroud into a treacherous handhold when going forward or boarding the yacht. They also obscure any defects that may be developing in rigging screw or terminal.

17 A good non-slip surface around the mast heel is essential, and footholds are desirable too.

18 A hatch garage not only prevents seeps around the fore end of a sliding hatch, but makes a handy site for a solar panel.

19 A length of strongly anchored Terylene webbing makes a good backrest if sitting on coaming or deck edge.

20 Make sure that the bilge pump is accessible – not sited in the depths of a locker!

21 Deep lockers that drain into the bilge, as many do, can be very dangerous to seagoing boats; ensure they are sealed internally and provided with a secure (and easy to operate) latch or toggles.

22 A tiller extension with universal joint is well worth having; make certain, though, that it is not too long or it may jam under a locker lip.

side of sailing and one that many people eventually come to enjoy. While it may take a while to establish a degree of sure-footedness and a good sense of balance if these do not come naturally, it really is worth persevering; to my mind, all members of the crew, except the very youngest, should be capable of foredeck work, for the time may come when the yacht's safety depends upon it. The old adage of 'one hand for yourself, one hand for the ship' should in heavy weather, though, perhaps be amended to 'both hands for yourself'! By the same token, there is no need (nor even much sense) in attempting to stand upright if the motion is violent – instead, go forward on hands and knees and dispense with any macho ideas!

The surface of the decks

The surface of the deck is at least as important as its actual area, and in this respect many modern GRP small yachts score poorly, with moulded 'non-slip' patterns in a variety of textures ranging from 'leather-look' to 'uncut moquette'; these are about as effective as the fabric from which the pattern was derived when they are new – and after a few seasons' wear, utterly useless. The aggressively textured 'Treadmaster' and its near relatives are very effective, though they are heavy and far from cheap. For this reason, on a small cruiser they are mainly used in small strips or panels and only in so-called traffic areas: in way of the mast, on the foredeck and sidedecks. (Beware, though, of using these on cockpit seats, for it will result in speedy erosion of any trousers with which they come into prolonged contact – I wore right through the seat of a pair of PVC trousers in the course of a Round-the-Island race!)

Sanded paint is cheap and works well enough – on timber as well as GRP – although some additional sand is best mixed even with the proprietary non-slip paint brands. Time and the passage of feet does wear this surface smooth, and it may need a fresh application every two years.

To those with a traditional turn of mind, it might seem a sin that many early wooden boats have had the original tongued-and-grooved decks sheathed in glassfibre, but this practice is by no means uncommon. It is certainly not to be recommended, since flexing of the seams will eventually crack the surface of the GRP and allow water to penetrate; but if sheathing is the only alternative to re-decking, seams should be splined and glued first. However, the idea of applying sheathing – or even paint – to a laid deck (a planked deck where each seam on the upper surface is payed with marine glue or sealant) is anathema. Leaving aside the fact that the natural scrubbed wood possesses first-rate anti-slip properties, the sheathing will not bond satisfactorily to the sealant; once again, water will permeate. A laid teak deck enhances the look of any boat, assuming that the timber is in fact 'tectona grandis'; several of the bastard species of timber, though superficially similar in appearance, are less durable and prone to splintering and discoloration. Teak strips can also be used to provide a foothold where most needed, although bonding to a glassfibre substrate is problematical. Another alternative, although one best suited to wooden yachts, is the employment of one of the pre-fabricated panel systems; the best of these (and hence the most expensive) are indistinguishable from the hand-crafted solid product, but how durable they prove in practice is open to doubt.

Plywood and tongued-and-grooved decks frequently rely upon a covering of painted canvas or the long-standing favourite: Trakmark – a textured composition surfaced fabric. Either of these, if carefully laid (all fittings, quadrants and beadings, as well as rubbing bands etc, should be removed prior to covering the decks), is workmanlike and economical – and both remain waterproof for years, unless physically damaged.

For a real sense of security when working on the foredecks or sidedecks, there is nothing to beat deep bulwarks, but these are ruled out for a small yacht where the height of topsides is a prime consideration. In both wooden and GRP small craft, they are also expensive to construct. However, the trendy alloy toe rails that also stiffen the hull/deck flange joint of a glassfibre boat, and provide anchorages for any wandering sheet blocks, are far too shallow to brace a foot against. Not that those toe rails moulded integrally with the decks of GRP yachts are much better; frequently they are laid up with so much outward curvature (and such a slippery finish) that they are worse than useless. Most smaller wooden boats rely only on fragile timber slips, an inch or so in height.

Are guardwires worth fitting?

Although there seems to be little inclination to improve the efficacy of the actual toe rails, there appears to be a firmly rooted belief that the provision of stanchions and lifelines constitutes a guarantee against going overboard. Unfortunately, it does not! To start with, many (if not all) of the sockets are very inadequately fastened – often by undersized bolts (or self-tapping screws) and have only a token backing pad, or occasionally none at all: certainly, few stanchions could be counted upon to withstand the weight of an adult thrown against them. Innovative thinking has caused designers to come up with attachment points other than the deck itself, with the upper edge of the moulded toe rail being a strong favourite; however, not only is the moulding generally weak here, being rich in resin and sparse in glass mat or roving, but if the stanchion base starts to move – and it eventually will – it is the devil's own job to get at the underside, repair the laminate and refasten the fitting.

At least where there is a straightforward bolt through to an internal pad, trouble can be dealt with as soon as it is detected (watch out for internal rust weeps and external craze lines in the case of a GRP boat, and delamination or eroded timber with a wooden one). Ironically, the stanchion sockets bolted through the aluminium rails are quite strong, though very prone to corrosion, and should one be damaged, any injury is usually limited to the fitment itself instead of also affecting the adjacent area of deck.

Failure of either the stanchions, sockets or deck is not, as a rule, brought about by thoughtless members of the crew hurling themselves against the lifelines over the side, but is likely to be sustained as a result of conflict with boatyard crane or travelhoist – or, more accurately, with the slings thereof; omitting to ease off the lifelines when lifting brings the pressure from the slings to bear directly on the lines, and hence also the stanchions. As many small yachts have a good deal of camber in the deck, the stanchions mounted directly on to it (rather than on blocks) tend to splay outwards; this is a nuisance when mooring alongside another boat, but especially vulnerable to strain during craneage. (Yet another cause of damage is using stanchion or lifeline as a handhold when boarding!)

Lifelines should be looked upon for reassurance but little else, and it is a popular misconception that double lines are necessarily doubly safe: even a substantial adult can quite easily slither through – and thence into the hoggin (as I know from bitter experience!). Such an eventuality could be prevented by ensuring that all the crew on deck or in the cockpit wear a safety harness and clip it on to a strong point or jackstay; however, there are times when this is not practicable, and human nature being what it is, there are occasions when a momentary panic causes forgetfulness. Also, mercifully rare though they are, emergencies can arise in which even the few seconds needed to hook on could conceivably endanger the

Boarding even a 19 footer from the tender can call for some agility; fortunately, in this case the dinghy is stable and the life-lines do not extend right aft – when they do, they should be fit-ted with a pelican hook so they can be freed off. Stress is a frequent cause of damage to the deck by way of the stanchion sockets.

yacht. There are also those crew members who are well accustomed to moving about on deck, possibly having spent years in offshore racing boats, and genuinely feel safer when working unencumbered by a harness and line. (And, as with stanchion sockets, jackstay attachment points are often not as strong as they ought to be – nor would I put total confidence in many of these – or the wire jackstays – I have seen.

As far as the small craft is concerned, there is one other dis-advantage to stanchions and lifelines, though it is one that would be contested. Given the narrow sidedecks of most small boats, the lifelines make it awkward to go forward since they are very apt to snag in clothing, particularly under jackets. The area of deck in way of the shrouds is especially restricted. In boats under 20 ft (6 m) or so, it makes far more sense to dis-pense with lifelines along sidedecks, and to fit a longer than standard pulpit that will offer increased protection on the fore-deck when struggling with headsails or mooring lines. A pul-pit really is indispensable for a cruising boat. (Having said that, yachts sailed around happily without these in Victorian times, and even a generation ago, those who first fitted a pulpit were regarded as of an unduly cowardly disposition!)

Strong grab rails on the coachroof are a must, though following 'big boat practice', they are rarely installed in the best place – all too often being fitted some distance inboard from the coachroof edge. Here they tend to be just out of reach of the grasping hand – or fumbling foot! It makes sense to extend the main hatch runners forward, at least to the mast, and fit the grab rail to the coachroof edge – especially useful is a strong rail, 3–6 in (7.6–15.2 cm) high, that encircles the mast heel; this gives a great sense of security when struggling with recalcitrant halyards and flogging sails (comes in handy, too, for tidying up all the lazy ends that accumulate round the mast).

Sooner or later, each and every fitment on deck is bound to serve as a foothold, whether meant to do so or not, therefore anything capable of giving under pressure – blocks or winches, for example – should, as far as is practicable, be kept away from traffic areas. This is much easier said than done on a small yacht, even one with a basic masthead sloop rig! By the same token, all items of deck hardware not intended to slide, pivot or rotate about the axis should be well and truly immovable!

The cockpit layout

Although an ergonomically laid-out cockpit is regarded as a good selling point, there is arguably more attention paid to comfort and efficiency where a boat is oriented to racing. Those who cruise are presumed to have become inured to discomfort, exposure to the elements, and not be over-preoccupied with such matters as the design and siting of sail controls. Whether a micro yacht is intended for racing or cruising, the transit point from cockpit to sidedeck (the after part of the sidedeck is generally at the narrowest point, cluttered with headsail tracks) is often awkward, requiring an undignified and precarious scramble: this is especially so where the coaming extends to the deck edge and 'wraps around' the fore part of the cockpit. Neither are matters improved by the conspicuous absence of grab rails within easy reach; and since it is rarely practicable to alter the coamings, the provision of substantial vertical rails on the main bulkhead could often be very helpful.

Depending upon design priorities, cockpits of individual small yachts could be expected to differ to an extent, but there should none the less be certain attributes in common: a

An excellent combined grab and foot rail around the mast on this small Danish keel boat.

footwell, wide but not too wide to brace against when the boat is heeled; a degree of protection afforded by coamings; and unimpeded forward visibility, even when the boat is level. Naturally, the cockpit should be self-draining. Or should it?

Personally, I think there is absolutely no doubt that it should be, but, surprisingly, there is a school of thought that argues the exact opposite. True, in the little traditional cruisers such as the Blackwater sloops and Deben Cherubs, it was next to impossible to combine a cockpit that self-drained with one deep enough to afford even an illusory sense of security to the crew. This is because in order to clear of water, the sole has to be above the waterline; since the freeboard of many older craft was inclined to be lower than on modern counterparts, the well would perforce be shallow and the crew faced with little alternative but to perch on the coamings if they felt the need to stretch their legs.

Usually, the cockpit sole consisted of loose laid planks, often unpainted; as the season progressed, though, the wood expanded as a result of damp and the boards tightened into place. However, they could never be thought of as watertight. Neither, in numerous older boats, is there a storm sill or bridgedeck separating the cabin from cockpit; often a pair of fragile hinged doors (sometimes opening inwards rather than outwards) was considered adequate, even for coastal and off-shore passages. This fact, though, gives rise to the second argument against the self-draining cockpit: should one of 'traditional' type be flooded, the water would pour through the sole (and also, presumably, the cabin doors) and into the main bilge, thus distributing the weight evenly throughout the boat. It was stoutly maintained that if and when this occurred, there would be a better chance of avoiding a second inundation than if the stern were to be pinned down by the 100 gallons or so of sea water confined within the watertight cockpit well – which would take minutes, at best, to evacuate through the scuppers. The argument is not without some validity, but personally I would prefer never to be forced to put the matter to the test. (And it also seems doubtful whether a petrol engine could be coaxed into life immediately afterwards – or, indeed, ever again!)

If the provision of a self-draining cockpit really is not viable, at the very least an attempt should be made to ensure that the well is watertight and can be pumped or bailed dry as quickly as possible. Even rainwater can be a serious threat where a small yacht is left unattended; the toughest fitted covers can break loose and shred in a storm. In the absence of a watertight cockpit, an owner would be well advised to install an electric bilge pump with automatic float switch (and ensure that the battery is kept fully charged).

With a traditional hull, achieving total watertight integrity is difficult and fitting bearers and sole to the frames is really a job for a shipwright. Yet any attempt is better than none – even the makeshift device of a heavy canvas internal cockpit liner, with a sturdy lifting handle on the centreline, so (in theory) water can be tipped back where it belongs, provides a degree of reassurance in heavy going.

A last complaint from the 'anti self-draining brigade' is that in order for the cockpit to drain, there must be scuppers fitted to the sole, and except in cases where they exit directly through the transom, this will mean hoses (which may have to cross over to avoid water sloshing back up *into* the cockpit when the boat heels) and it will also entail drilling holes in the hull! (And all underwater discharges must be fitted with seacocks or gate valves, although, so far as cockpit drain outlets are concerned, this stipulation is, on micro yachts anyway, more honoured in the breach than the observance.) Some small boats fit manually operated self-bailers in conjunction with a watertight sole, and very irritating these can be – as every dinghy sailor learns: they leak, jam open (or jam closed, depending on which is the most inconvenient) and are easily damaged. Also, they will not operate at speeds much below 4 knots, and few small cruisers rarely attain racing dinghy speeds!

The capacity and siting of cockpit lockers, is (or should be) an

The Nimrod. A little over 17 ft (5.1 m) in length, it was originally designed to be sailed dinghy fashion with the crew comfortably perched on the sidedecks, feet under toe straps. One or two of today's more extreme racing micros are powered along with helmsman and crew on trapezes!

integral part of the design. However, sometimes it appears to be no more than an afterthought: if there's a vacant space, large or small, beneath a sidebench, under the sole, jammed into the stern, then there's room for a locker – regardless of the size and weight of the contents or access in emergency. Space is very much at a premium on the small yacht, and the items that can realistically be stowed only in the cockpit take up a higher proportion of available room than on a bigger vessel.

Open transoms

Open transoms, once regarded as suitable only for racing dinghies (and extreme ones at that), are now fashionable for numerous larger sailcraft; this format, while clearing any serious water from the cockpit, does ensure a more or less constant gentle ebb and flow of damp around the feet of the crew; one lapse of concentration and this peaceable current turns into a flood. Therefore, as long as the yacht has way on and those aboard concentrate the collective mind on correct weight distribution (in other words, don't allow the transom to become even partly immersed), the cockpit should stay relatively clear of water – and this without any need for scuppers or skin fittings. However, an open stern only functions properly if planned at the design stage: hacking away the transom of a narrow-beamed, heavier yacht that does not have a completely flat run aft is pointless.

Though the very simplicity of the concept could be considered an asset, there are structural drawbacks: backstays and the outboard motor mounting (and frequently the rudder too) all have to be tacked on to the after end somehow, and options are pretty restricted with this type of stern; often, after only a season's use, clear evidence of stress may be visible in way of fittings so that refastening is necessary – and possibly reinforcement, which could be unsightly.

It should not be forgotten that, once sailing hard, anything that can be washed aft and through the transom will be – so all odds and sods of gear should be tucked well away; the same goes for sheet tails, loose lines, fenders etc, all of which will stream merrily astern to snarl with propeller, log line or each other; netting will help to prevent this, but the mesh must be quite closely woven to be of much use. (Even in port, an unguarded open transom seems to exercise a powerful attraction for small children or seagoing pets – so watch out that there is no opportunity for these to make an unscheduled exit.)

Assuming that the full complement of crew does remain within the cockpit, they will appreciate the difference that a sidebench, contoured to that portion of the anatomy with which it comes into closest contact, can make to a cruise. Flat bench tops, often too wide or narrow (especially flat seats with overlaid teak slats or gratings), produce, among other well-documented symptoms, a nagging backache after only a couple of hours unless there is an opportunity to change position or posture – and this may not be practicable. Early yachts paid little attention to the matter of lumbar support – sailing was,

The simply laid-out cockpit of an E-boat – ideal for racing as the crew can get the weight well outboard, but rather exposed when cruising as there are no coamings.

after all, intended to build up the character! However, during the transitional period from the use of wood to glassfibre in boatbuilding, the influence of racing dinghies changed that attitude somewhat; small and very fast boats with weekending accommodation – such as the Nimrod and the Allegro – featured rolled sidedecks and, to complete the illusion of dinghy sailing, the crew tucked their feet under toe straps and hiked out. This is not, incidentally, nearly so gruelling as it sounds – at least, not once the stomach muscles become hardened to it (it can be hell during the weeks of acclimatisation though!). The toe straps, it goes without saying, must be of really heavy-duty webbing, with all attachment points and through-fastenings checked. Should a toe strap come adrift on board a dinghy, it's rather embarrassing – the crew will summarily part company with the boat and capsize will follow immediately after; however, the consequences if sailing a cruiser offshore could be fatal, since the yacht would probably maintain course for some distance, *sans* occupants! So if sailing in this fashion (and it can be very rewarding in settled weather), don't sail with sheets cleated, and *never* with the autopilot set.

Box section coamings, wide enough to double as winch platform and additional crew seating, really are a great asset to the small boat – whether racing or cruising. Perched on the coaming top, forward visibility is usually excellent, even under a low-cut genoa: if the coamings are too narrow for comfort, those in the know often knock together a simple demountable stool that drops into place over the top; for those too lazy to construct two, setting it up on the weather side becomes another chore on changing tack! For that matter, a more sophisticated fixed outboard seat, such as that offered with the JOG version of the 19 ft (5.7 m) plywood Caprice in the late 1960s, is quite easy for the amateur to construct; but even the simpler alternative of laminating a wider external coaming lip does provide a handy parking spot for short-term use. Given a wide box section, whether of GRP or timber construction, cave lockers can be recessed into it (prefabricated edging and lining kits for this purpose are widely available). These are invaluable: sail ties, notebooks, winch handles and all the impedimenta that accumulate on a cruise can be tidied out of the way.

Auxiliary power

The majority of small yachts rely for auxiliary propulsion on an outboard motor rather than an inboard installation; sometimes this is a matter of preference, occasionally of practicality. It is, for example, inadvisable to fit an inboard to a flush-bottomed lift-keel boat that regularly takes the ground, because without protection for the sterngear, this is very susceptible to damage. Cost may conceivably be a factor too, but often an inboard is ruled out on the grounds of size and weight – although there are several suitable petrol and petroil engines available (the RCA Dolphin, the 4 hp Stuart Turner and the Watermota Shrimp, to name but three) that turn the scales at rather less than an average adult crew member. Even where a model is not in current production, spares are quite easily obtained, and once their idiosyncrasies are understood, the engines, which are mechanically simple, are quite reliable (though Stuarts have attained cult status with acolytes spending much time on bended knees before them!). However, the fire hazard has focused attention on diesels even though the most compact of these would be a tight fit on a micro yacht and might also adversely affect performance.

Modern outboards are sophisticated pieces of engineering and can offer many of the functions associated with an inboard, such as running the lighting or charging batteries. Less oil-rich mixtures mean that spark plugs are less inclined to foul, so starting, fuel economy and general reliability are much enhanced. Increased use of plastics and aluminium ensure remarkable power-to-weight ratios and an up-to-date

6 hp motor – about right as auxiliary for a yacht of 18–22 ft (5.4–6.7 m) (depending on the boat's displacement and hull configuration) – weighs in the region of 70 lb (32 kg). No great weight certainly, but when an outboard is transom mounted, it is weight in the least desirable place. This being so, many people prefer to remove the outboard when sailing, and it is a cussed object to stow securely, unless there is a specific cockpit locker for it. Often there is not, the assumption being that the unit will be tucked beneath the fixed cockpit sole or left in the cabin during sailing. Yet apart from the physical difficulty of manoeuvring an outboard, even a short shaft, in a confined space, with even the cleanest and most carefully maintained engine there is always a little fuel spillage – messy, smelly and slippery underfoot!

If an outboard is to function as an auxiliary in the fullest sense of the word, rather than merely to nudge the boat into a marina berth or stem a foul tide, it must be capable of operating for at least a couple of hours without the need for refuelling (this might be a highly fraught undertaking if the outboard is running in anything of a sea), to claw off a lee shore for example, or return to a safe haven after an emergency – perhaps after losing mast or rudder. This being so, the engine is best fed from a separate remote tank with a capacity usually of either 2 or 5 gals (9–22 l) (standard with many, though not all, engines over 6 hp). Ideally, this tank should be stowed in a dedicated locker, where it can remain during use. Unfortunately, little provision is made for this; so often, with the tank stowed, the fuel line cannot reach the outboard, and there is no alternative to depositing it on the cockpit sole. Yet, no matter what the siting, the tank must always be retained securely, for should it move around, there is every chance that the fuel line might disconnect, pinch closed, or otherwise suffer injury.

Needless to say, if spare petrol is taken on board, it must be carried in approved containers, preferably the type with internal expanded mesh that guards against explosion, and all cans must be secured against the movements of the yacht in heavy weather! (For siting outboards see p 57.)

Gas stowage requirements

The regulations pertaining to the installation and carriage of LPG (liquid petroleum gas) on board yachts have become stringent, and failure to conform with the current regulations might invalidate any insurance claim (even a claim with which the gas installation was totally unconnected). The gas cylinder, fitted with the approved regulator, must be stowed in an upright position, in a locker above the waterline and securely retained. The locker must be completely separate, and fitted with an overside drain (to allow the gas, which is heavier than air, to be dispersed overboard in the event of cylinder spillage). Relatively few older craft comply with this requirement (and, surprisingly, neither do all modern ones), so if this is the case, construction of a suitable locker above the waterline level must be regarded as a priority job, along with provision of rigid copper piping and approved reinforced and/or armoured hose (the hose employed must be of the minimum practicable lengths) from regulator to gas-burning units. It is generally possible to partition off and seal a section of a larger locker, and if there is a self-draining cockpit, a storage locker could possibly be contained within the well, with any gas dispersing overboard via cockpit drains. True, this could restrict footroom in the average small yacht, and only where the cockpit is unusually long in proportion or extends right aft to the transom would this option be worth thinking about, although it might be possible to incorporate cylinder storage with a removable thwartships seat. Another option, if the cockpit is divided by the mainsheet track, is to fabricate a locker beneath this. The cylinder can also be stowed on deck or on the coachroof; although bearing in mind the need to keep weight as low as possible, this is hardly a viable option for a small yacht.

Although with boats increasingly moored in close proximity in marinas and crowded harbours the risk of mass damage through a single explosion has greatly increased, LPG is not, per se, dangerous – so long as it is used with common sense. Indeed, it could be argued that it is the best fuel for cooking on a small boat, and superior to alcohol or pressure paraffin when under way because of its cleanliness, ease of use and calorific efficiency. Not everyone is, in fact, unreservedly in favour of the current regulations: for a start, there is an argument that the siting of the gas bottle as close as possible to the appliance must be safer if only because the crew, faced with a sortie aft to turn off the supply at the cylinder (perhaps in a downpour), may simply decide not to bother. No one, though, can prevent laziness by legislation! Another point, which does have some validity, is the inaccessibility of the copper pipework from cylinder to appliance; often the tube vanishes from sight into GRP accommodation modules, and so renders inspection impossible. However, nothing lasts for ever, especially in a marine environment. Therefore, all connections from the cylinder to the cooker, as well as the reinforced and/or armoured hose and hose clips, must be inspected as a routine part of the annual maintenance, and be replaced at the slightest sign of deterioration, chafe or corrosion.

The bilge pump

Obviously, safe stowage of and access to such potentially hazardous substances as fuel and gas, which can endanger the boat, are of paramount importance, but equally vital is the situation and ease of operation of the bilge pump – which might equally well save it!

When it comes to the bilge pump, in smaller yachts at least, there seems to be a noticeable preoccupation with tucking the object out of harm's way (hoping against hope that it will never be used in earnest, perhaps?) and it is often doubtful whether the crew will be able to operate it efficiently (or at all) in time of need. The favourite hiding place is deep within a sidebench locker or aft lazarette, and both are pretty hopeless: usually the locker lid must be propped or held open while pumping – not an onerous undertaking if all that is involved is clearing an inch or two of rain or spray from the bilge, but a very different matter in the event of a torrential ingress of water, as there would be if damage to the underbody is sustained. (Quite apart from anything else, that raised lid could mean all normal activity in the cockpit would have to be suspended – and an open lazarette lid would be quite likely to restrict helm movement as well.)

Through-deck (or bulkhead) operation is available on many of the diaphragm pumps now so widely used, and this is close to the ideal – with the caveat that the pump and hoses remain within reach for regular inspection.

That the highly efficient diaphragm bilge pump has largely superseded the reciprocating and semi-rotary types is hardly surprising: diaphragm pumps, which may have single or double action, are both effort- and cost-effective, and virtually impossible to choke (if this does happen, they are not difficult to clear – though the process can take a few minutes' fiddling). The inlet should always be provided with a strum box (strainer), but it is astonishing just how often this gets overlooked. Even the best maintained boat can accumulate remarkable quantities of debris, paper pulp, etc in the bilges, and this may escape notice if the entire cabin sole is screwed into place (which it shouldn't be, but frequently is). A strum box is the best single guarantee that the pump will work when needed – although it's a cast iron certainty that without one, the pump will choke at the most inconvenient moment. If that does happen – well, the old cliché that a panic-stricken crew member, armed with a bucket, will chuck water overboard faster than any pump invented will soon be put to the test!

Diaphragm pumps have a well-deserved reputation for long life and, unlike the old semi-rotary types, they work on the first pull of the handle, without any need for priming. Rarely do they fail for structural reasons, but in the smallest models it is not unknown for the plastic handle to break – and an instant repair may be out of the question. Also, over a period of years, the diaphragm (of neoprene or nitrile rubber), though tough and resilient, will eventually perish; and as with so many equipment failures, if this happens, it is bound to happen in an emergency!

Reliable as diaphragm pumps are, even the smallest yacht should carry a back-up; unfortunately, relatively few do – unless club or offshore racing rules demand it. What strains credulity, though, is the number of vessels that put to sea without even one (indeed, without even so much as a Mark I bucket to bless themselves with!). Ideally, each pump should be provided with an inlet hose (with strum box) capable of reaching both the cockpit bilge and main cabin bilge space – larger craft often have twin pumps with a diverter valve, so each can substitute for the other should the need arise.

As is the case with just about each and every aspect of yacht design, opinions diverge about cockpit lockers – not just about the siting, but whether or not there should actually be any. Certainly, unless each locker is individually separated from the bilge, deep lockers can be a hazard at sea; and while there is no great difficulty achieving a watertight seal where the craft is built of marine ply or GRP, with traditional build it is not so straightforward. In reality, as with so many other things appertaining to the small yacht, provision of locker space comes a poor second to fitting in the required number of berths: this means in practice that where there are two quarter berths running under the sidebenches, there cannot be cockpit lockers of any great capacity. Now while this is an excellent arrangement in so far as regards absolute and continued watertight integrity in heavy weather, it is less than ideal for a cruising boat, since every item that must not – or should not – be stowed below decks (ie fuel, gas, fenders, warps and kedge anchor (the last three ought to be ready for immediate use at all times) has to be crammed into the lazarette (if there is one – for obvious reasons, an aft locker cannot be combined with an open transom!). Bear in mind, too, that contained within this locker will be the gas cylinder (stowed in a separate compartment), and also one, possibly two, fuel tanks. Clearly, there will be little space left over for warps, fenders and general items, and none whatsoever for an inflatable dinghy – which would have to be partially deflated and carried on the coachroof when cruising, inflatables not being especially renowned for tractability under tow!

Siting the outboard

Unless the outboard is installed within a well or trunking, there will be little alternative to leaving it in situ on the transom – possibly even when the vessel is lying unattended on a mooring or marina berth – but remember that outboard motors are like magnets to thieves, who go to almost any lengths to steal them. Naturally, the engine would be secured against such an eventuality by chain – toughened chain at that – made fast through the bracket, but even this will not defeat a determined criminal: it has been known for the engine to be removed by hacking through the bracket with a chainsaw (needless to say, large chunks of transom went with it).

An outboard well, though offering an illusory guarantee against theft (it really is little more than this, although there is a sporting chance that the opportunist thief might not actually realise that there is an engine beneath the hatch), is, so far as the general stowage space is concerned, not an unmixed

A well-designed outboard stowage locker, the lid fitted with seals and toggle closure.

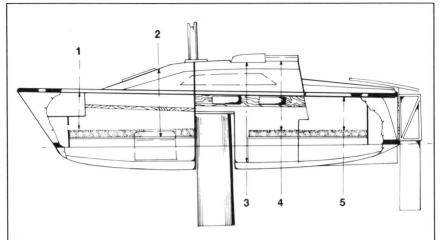

Accommodation

Reconciling a seaworthy hull design, good performance on all points of sailing with acceptable accommodation below calls for all the designer's skill and ingenuity – especially when shallow or variable draft is a requisite. A layout that is quite acceptable in harbour or on a mooring, with the craft on an even keel, may not work so well at sea. Neither can the human figure be relied upon to fit neatly into its designed space (at least, not if it is subject to restless sleeping or untidy sprawling), so quarter berths, berths in 'trotter boxes' and pilot berths may be untenable except by junior members of the crew.

The accommodation plans and section of a fairly typical 20 ft (6 m) lift-keeler, with the galley constructed around the keel box, show approximate heights and widths needed for an average-sized adult to exist without undue discomfort.

1 Footroom underneath anchor locker is essential: minimum 12 in (30 cm).

2 Headroom over toilet (ideally the forehatch should open and give a bit more room): minimum 3 ft (91 cm).

3 Standing room is always diminished slightly by linings and positioning of cabin soles, and in many small GRP yachts the inside of the hull is itself the sole; in wooden boats, angled or curved soles may be employed to make the most use of available space. If full headroom cannot be achieved, there is little gain in struggling to obtain it, settle for good sitting headroom, 4 ft–5 ft is about the best to be expected from a 20 footer – and even this will be at the cost of bulky topsides.

4 Sitting headroom must take into account the thickness of berth cushions, and also allowance must be made for berth sole boards or webbing. It is not easy to achieve sitting headroom under the sidedecks of a small yacht, and the space might best be occupied by fitted lockers: minimum 3 ft 6 in (1 m).

5 Hip room at the dividing bulkhead of a quarter berth – this can make all the difference for a restless sleeper. Nearly all quarter berths and those run in trunkings or trotter boxes are short on this – this is OK for an exhausted offwatch crew perhaps, but hardly enjoyable in the longer term: minimum 22 in (56 cm).

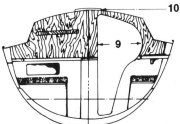

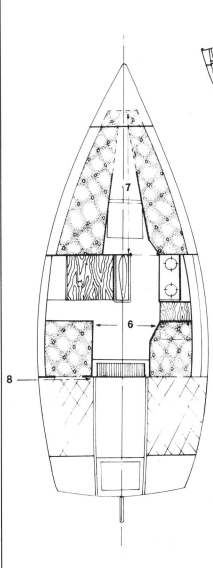

6 Knee room across the sole is critical for those at the dining table; since table dimensions are also likely to be minimal in a micro cruiser, it may be a better idea to eat off individual folding tables or trays: ideal 50 in (127 cm).

7 Length of bunks is important, but there is rarely any need for more than two over 6 ft (1.8 m) in overall length. Some quarter berths in small boats approach 7 ft (2.1 m) and the space might be better taken up with watertight cockpit lockers: minimum two at 6 ft (1.8 m), one at 6 ft 3 in (1.9 m) (fourth can usually be smaller if necessary).

8 Width, however, is important: a narrow berth into which the sleeper can wedge securely is a blessing at sea, although less so in harbour. Double berths in particular are useless under way unless they can be divided with a lee cloth.

9 Shoulder room for access in bulkheads: minimum 20 in (51 cm).

10 Dimensions of a hatch intended to allow escape in the event of an emergency – and the importance of a second hatch cannot be too highly stressed: minimum 20 in (51 cm) measured diagonally.

blessing – after all, fit a well and there is no possibility of an after locker with sensible dimensions. Yet so far as engine performance and efficiency go, there are distinct advantages: for a start, the weight of the engine is slightly further forward, which makes an appreciable difference to trim, particularly in the narrower, counter-sterned boats that typified the earlier micro yachts. Even more important is the fact that the engine is subjected to less pitching when installed forward of the transom, and pitching, with attendant cavitation of the propeller, is anathema to the small craft: each time the bows bury in a sea, the propeller is flung clear to race wildly – not greatly productive of forward motion nor especially good for the engine!

Older outboards with oil-rich fuel mixtures always had a reputation for running erratically (or not at all) when installed in a trunking, with opinion at the time suggesting that the engines literally choked on their own fumes. It seems more likely, though, that not enough attention was paid to the correct shaft length, for it is essential that the shaft is not immersed too deeply. If there is any doubt about this, consult the outboard manufacturers or agents. Incidentally, where the boat is flush bottomed, with a lift keel or centreplate, for example, remember to lift the engine prior to taking the ground – for some reason, once in that well, it is too easy to think of it as a permanent fixture.

One good-sized locker (although not essential) is a useful asset, but with the proviso that it must be a separate and watertight entity, sealed from cockpit and main bilge alike. Though designers as a rule appreciate the importance of this, they forget to convey their opinion to the builders, who reckon that the deeper the locker, the better, and thus cheerfully leave the lower section unsealed. Some of the blame is admittedly down to owners; without a thought of possible consequences, they delight in cutting holes through the accommodation bulkheads to run hoses or pipework through, or perhaps to give access to an inboard engine. In certain designs, the all-important dividing bulkhead between the cockpit and accommodation loses watertight integrity by having access hatches cut through at settee level, so the contents of the cockpit locker are within handy reach of the occupants of the cabin. Hatches tend to be whimsical little constructions of 3 mm plywood (even hardboard), with only the most primitive form of retention (although once upholstered and trimmed, there is the spurious suggestion of solidity).

Very few people are unfortunate enough to undergo a knock-down, swamping or the dubious pleasure of having a following sea join them in the cockpit, but in any of these circumstances, the force of the inrush is immense: should a locker lid carry away and water find its way into cockpit bilge and accommodation, a merely unpleasant scenario could be transformed into one of disaster. Compromise here, as in so many matters, is the best course.

The quarter berths, even on small craft, can be as much as a couple of feet longer than is strictly necessary (few family cruising boats have more than one crew member over 6 feet (1.8 m) tall), and that redundant mattress space could instead provide a small cockpit locker suitable for gas or fuel; because of the additional cost factor, though, this rarely seems to be considered viable in the case of production boats.

Surprisingly, even where lockers are so large or ill-designed that inundation could bring about the yacht's demise, sealing strips are not necessarily fitted, and the means of securing the lid is often inadequate; in fact, there may be nothing more than the lid's own weight to keep it closed. Toggles or hasps and staples (the latter can be padlocked against possible pilferage) are best, even though these can catch in oilskins. A line running from the underside of the lid to a cleat inside the cabin is often employed to good effect, but is difficult to reach from the cockpit (with possible serious consequences if, for instance, flares or similar items of equipment for emergency use are stowed within it!).

Hatches and windows

All locker lids and hatches (and windows too) have an essential role in assuring the continued watertight integrity – and thus the seaworthiness – of the vessel. When a yacht founders, it is likely to be the result of a combination of circumstances rather than a single error of judgement or the failure of one item of gear. Yet with many casualties, a hatch or window is cited as a major contributory cause, either because it has carried away or was not secured by the crew; it is easy to blame those on board for wanton carelessness, but sometimes there just is no warning of a 'rogue wave' or veering gust that can bring about a broach and knock-down.

Since the dimensions of the human frame don't obligingly diminish in accordance with the boat size, the accommodation access hatches take up a disproportionally large area of the deck of a small yacht (because of the beast's relatively low freeboard, they are under flying spray for an unduly large part of the time too!). It would be reasonable to assume that hatch sizes would be kept to the minimum practicable size for

The Hardy 21 motorsailer – an attractive compromise with an acceptable performance under sail, but it also has a powerful engine, nearly full headroom in the wheelhouse – and an inside steering position for those cold wet days of summer!

an adult to use, and that both the hatch and deck or coachroof area in the immediate vicinity would be heavily reinforced; however, production costs (and, an earnest desire to keep down the weight of the superstructure) mean that this is not universal practice.

As a rule, the main hatch is the largest on the yacht – and, of course, the most frequently used. Modern preference seems to be for ever-larger main hatches and, on occasion, for a unit that can be removed completely: to facilitate sail trimming or, used in conjunction with a boom tent, to increase headroom below decks. The fact that such oversized (and usually under-weight) hatches are a potential source of danger seems to pass largely unremarked.

Of course, an attempt to combine the ability to slide freely (or tilt or fold as the case may be) with total watertight integrity is a challenge, and it is one that few light glassfibre or acrylic panel hatches meet in a satisfactory manner; those that slide within runners (instead of being constructed with an external overlap) always allow a few weeps and dribbles below – whether in open or closed position. Building a hatch garage, even a light one of marine ply or GRP, goes a long way to eliminate leaks. It also provides a good protected site for a solar panel, and also for an instrument housing on the after edge.

Whatever the construction material, the main hatch must be sturdy enough to withstand an adult's weight without risk of breakage, and must operate with minimal friction: stainless steel external runners are far and away the best, for timber tends to swell and jam when damp, and GRP rarely allows a close fit. Also, the hatch must be capable of being secured in place even (especially, in fact) if the yacht is inverted or rolled. Obviously the same applies to flushing boards too, and there are well-thought-out designs (albeit usually only on larger off-shore cruising boats) that overlap the flushing boards or doors and keep these in position if the worst happens. The crew must be able to open, or remove, the boards easily when necessary from either the cockpit and accommodation, and if no other provision is made for this, an internal/external line passing through the upper section of the board is a simple and effec-tive method of retention. One single washboard is arguably more secure than two or three smaller ones; unquestionably, it is quicker to slot into place – those cunningly contrived boards that are tailored and rebated to fit in one position only are awkward at the best of times.

Ultimately, no matter how thorough the equipping of the yacht, or how comprehensive the inventory, safety rests in the hands of the crew. Preparations for a storm – stowing loose gear, having flares to hand and securing hatches – means fac-ing up to the possibility of a knock-down, and this is not always an easy thing to do: the skipper may need all the optimism and reassurance at his or her disposal if those on board show signs of alarm at such precautions.

The forehatch

The forehatch (which must always open aft, ie with the hinge or hinges on the forward edge) should be constructed on similarly robust lines to the main hatch, and should also be capable of secure retention from inside the cabin. Most timber hatches found in earlier production craft were well up to standard in these respects, but there are numerous GRP fabrications – once again dating from the 'experimental' period of volume boatbuilding – that are now in a very sorry state, with damage and heavy crazing manifest around all hinges and fastenings; in such a case as this, the hatch must be reinforced prior to any coastal sailing. Hatches or skylights with a translucent panel – be it of acrylic or toughened glass – ought to be provided with protective bars, for neither material is immune to impact. Regardless of whether they are constructed of wood, glassfibre or aluminium alloy, deck or coachroof hatches should be on the centreline of the yacht to minimise the possibility of immersion. The strongest – and most resistant to leaks – are the double-coaming type, and if flush fitting so as to offer minimal resistance to waves sweeping over, so much the better.

While structural weakness in a forehatch or its hinge and fastenings is not impossible to put right, one problem common to many small craft can be almost insurmountable – namely, the total absence of said fitment.

It was widely held – presumably by those who had not attempted it in bad weather – that the open forehatch made a secure retreat from which to set and dowse the headsails, an idea that nowadays has rather lost credibility (hardly surprising, since all such sail changes would be accompanied by liberal douches of cold water). Certainly, handing the sails through the forehatch is safer and easier than dragging them along the length of the sidedeck, but in a piping breeze solid water would find its way below. At anchor, an open forehatch provides welcome ventilation, but its vital function is as a means of emergency escape – in particular, escape from a fire. No one who has experienced a fire within the confines of a small cabin is likely to forget it. Because of the layout of the cruising yacht, a conflagration nearly always breaks out in the engine space – immediately below the companion – or, more commonly, in the galley; in either site, exit by way of the main hatch is effectively blocked. If the fire cannot be extinguished and there is no other hatch, there will be no way out – rarely do micro yachts have windows large enough for an adult to squeeze through, even if the glass or acrylic window panels could be broken quickly enough to allow escape. It has to be accepted that the retro-fitting of a forehatch to a glassfibre boat is difficult and not a job for an amateur – in certain boats, the actual design of the deck and superstructure will rule it out anyway. Should it really prove to be out of the question, great care has to be taken in siting the cooking stove: it must be well forward of the main hatch so that the cook is always working with a clear line of retreat behind. Cookers immediately adjacent to the main hatch, or that slide, fold or hinge into the bridgedeck or quarter berth, are dangerous and should be banned.

All hatches in the deck or coachroof are a potential source of weakness, as are cabin windows – and through-hull windows are worst of all. Inadvisable on a larger cruising boat, these can be dangerous on the small craft: if a knock-down occurs and the boat is pinned down with topsides submerged (as it might well happen in a broach under spinnaker), it has been estimated that within the space of ten seconds, as much as a metric tonne of water could be shipped through a breached window only a foot square – the force and quantity depending upon the immersed depth of the aperture.

Coachroof and through-hull windows

Not only cabin windows, but also those in topsides, are increasingly likely to be the overlaid type, with an acrylic panel through-bolted on to sealant – and often so heavily tinted that there doesn't seem a lot of point in fitting them in any case! Although such windows tend to be regarded as a bit of a design gimmick, they can be far superior to the 'conventional' type inset to coachroof or hull and secured with internal and external frames. Appearance is a matter of personal opinion, but the overlaid panels are well in keeping with the stark, pared-down lines of modern GRP yachts – in particular, those wishing to project a sporty image! However, they do very little to enhance a classic timber yacht.

As has been pointed out, the overlaid window has much to recommend it, the actual aperture is not too large and the amount of overlay is sufficient. (Also, assuming that the windows have in fact been through-bolted: it is not unknown for self-tapping screws to be used instead, even by professional builders!)

The state of hatches and windows requires careful monitoring – eternal vigilance being the price of peace of mind. Aluminium external frames corrode, eventually allowing water to seep through the joined extrusions, and sealants solidify and crack. Since every yacht hull, deck and superstructure is liable to flex to some degree, stress crazes may, in a glassfibre boat, become apparent in the vicinity of the window. These should be taken very seriously with a through-hull window. In the case of timber craft, rot or delamination will set in under a poorly sealed unit.

When sailing offshore, it is strongly advised that storm boards be fitted to all windows (and deadlights to opening ports). The former is not always practicable for the smaller yacht; in fact, the curvature of coachroof sides – and the lack of space – really rules out the use of easily demountable boards, and there will be little alternative to bolting on semi-permanent fitments. For normal coastal and 'home trade' limits (Elbe to Brest) voyaging, it probably makes better sense to ensure that windows are structurally 'above spec' and well maintained.

Certainly, the 'chicken coop' skylights, so beloved of the traditionalist, are not to be recommended in a small yacht – some quite tiny craft do sport them as a point of honour, but they are vulnerable to damage both from feet and breaking seas. Even sealing them against spray or rain is virtually impossible, and those jaunty little canvas covers don't offer much protection in heavy weather.

It's probably safe to say that no sailing yachts under 22 ft (6.7 m) overall have been designed with any kind of fixed shelter for the helmsman (though undoubtedly, on looking around, one or two have suffered the indignity of having such grafted on), but a spray hood improves life in the cockpit no end – so long as it does not impede forward visibility under way or when manoeuvring in harbour (and some quite definitely do).

3   A Basic Outline

Considering that the mast, rigging and sails of a yacht constitute the motive power, it is astonishing how frequently even the most basic maintenance may be ignored.

Apart from the 'alternative' rigs that now proliferate – wishbone, Chinese lug, wing and Freedom, not to mention such esoterica as kites or rotor systems – there is now considerable diversity in the design of the Bermudan sloop. This rig, still the most widely employed on both cruising and racing boats, sets just two working sails, the mainsail and foresail. It is efficient, particularly on the wind, and in theory it is simply stayed and easy to handle – with the emphasis on 'in theory'. The Bermudan sloop has undergone many changes since its inception at the turn of the century: originally the forestay extended perhaps to three-quarters of the total mast height (hence a relatively small headsail and large main), but this gradually gave way to the masthead rig, with the foresail, as would be surmised, carried right up to the mast truck. In recent years, the rig has, so to speak, come full circle – and now the three-quarter, or seven-eighths, rig (the fractional rig) is becoming the norm.

In early versions, the proportions of fore to mainsail were not too dissimilar to those of the gaff rig that the Bermudan supplanted, and although any fractional rig demanded fairly complex standing and running rigging, compared with the gaff it was simplicity itself. At that time, simply altering the fore-and-aft rake of the mast was considered quite daring, and was certainly tuning enough for any cruising boat.

The masthead Bermudan rig, as popularised in the small yacht, is uncomplicated, requires minimal standing rigging (and no running backstays or braces), and is arguably far better suited to a cruiser than the fractional counterpart. A number of drawbacks are cited, but perhaps these have more to do with fashion than common sense. Masthead rig, when it first came into widespread use in the 1960s, drew more than its fair share of criticism: it was held to be stumpy and distinctly 'unyachty'! Just the same, there was plentiful advice on beefing up the tapering spar associated with fractional rig so as to convert it to masthead – advantages clearly being thought to outweigh the aesthetics!

True, in the case of a masthead rigged cruiser, the mast may

When short tacking up a narrow channel a large overlapping headsail is more of a hindrance than a help – hence the increasing popularity of self-tacking headsails with a short foot and relatively small sail area. Note the mainsheet on a long strop, the idea being to reduce the amount of rope necessary and also to cut down on the lazy end in the cockpit when on the wind.

be rather shorter in comparison with the overall length of the boat (hence the 'stumpy' epithet attached to the rig by purists), and this is because, with more sail area forward of the mast, and a longer headsail luff (giving superior windward performance), it is possible to cut down the designed working sail area slightly. This is ideal for any cruiser – since the mast cannot be reefed along with the sails, excessive height (and weight) aloft are no great asset. Ironically, detractors claim that the masthead rig is unsuitable for short-handed sailing and that the large working headsail – usually of near equal size to the main, and occasionally (when taken to extremes) exceeding it – requires not only powerful winches, but split-second timing and a degree of brute force when short tacking. There is perhaps an element of truth in this, and unless some thought is given to siting of cleats etc on mast as well as fore-deck, it is not difficult for the sail to snag and catch aback. Neither of these irritations should trouble a practised crew, and in moderate airs the rig is usually tolerant of a slightly smaller than standard working jib. However, this in itself calls forth yet more vociferous argument from the fractional faction: the cost of and space occupied by a large number of headsails of sizes appropriate to all wind strengths. Undoubtedly, to maintain optimal performance on all points of sailing – as a racing boat would aim to do – there will be times when lively sail changes are the order of the day. Three headsails, possibly four, if a cruising chute, spinnaker or drifter is added to the wardrobe, will be needed but then, in order to get the most from a three-quarter rigged yacht, a full complement of head-sails would still be advisable!.

There is, however, no question that the small mainsail of a masthead Bermudan sloop, set as it is on a short boom, is both easier to reef when necessary (and, by the same token, will not so often need to be reefed) than in a fractional yacht of similar size – and not even slab or reefing with lazyjacks has taken all the hassle out of reducing the mainsail area when required. Also, an unscheduled gybe is less traumatic with a short, light boom!

Headsail changing and furling gears

Unless the accent is on competition, a storm jib and a working headsail will be sufficient for daysailing and short coastal pas-sages; however, the myth of an 'ongoing headsail change sit-uation' persists, and with it the constant search for ways in which to lighten the life of the foredeck hand.

Twin forestays, side by side, have always been popular with offshore voyagers, since a double-stay arrangement speeds up headsail changes – and is also an asset when setting twin-running foresails for trade wind sailing. Assuming that the stays are in fact duplicated and therefore completely indepen-dent of one another, ie individually attached to masthead and stemhead fittings, twins contribute greatly to the integrity of the rig; after all, the forestay and cap shrouds are, with a conventional Bermudan rig, the most important items of stand-ing rigging. As always, though, expense enters into the calcu-lations and a true twin system will probably entail custom fittings at masthead and deck level, so a compromise is arrived at: joining the forestays by spreader plates at top and bottom with these carried on to single fittings. While this does-n't do much to strengthen the rig, it still makes possible the main object of the exercise: that of being able to set one sail while the other (perhaps the storm jib) is stowed, but remains hanked on to the sister stay and ready to set immediately. (When passage making, this sail may be kept on the foredeck in a specially designed heavyweight bag that clips along the rail.) Such a system does cut down the time the crew has to spend in lonely exile on the foredeck, but unfortunately there is a slight, and inevitable, decrease in windward efficiency – though it is doubtful if it would be noticeable when cruising. This loss of edge occurs because of the difficulty of adequately tensioning the forestay (and the sail will lose even more drive if set on the leeward stay). One way of partly overcoming this is to incorporate a swivel to the joining spreaders so that, when in use, the forestays are lined up fore-and-aft with the operative sail always set on the after one, though this is arguably nothing more than another complication – one more item capable of jamming or seizing.

Some increase in drag is unavoidable with any twin fore-sail configuration, and as a consequence a single forestay fit-ted with an enveloping aerodynamic headfoil of aluminium alloy or plastic became the order of the day on racing boats. Essentially, little more than a sophisticated updating of the old theme, the headfoil consists of a light luff spar, but with twin grooves that enable one sail to be set while another is low-ered. The streamlined section of the foil minimises drag, and since the sail is set within the groove, there is no need to fiddle around with recalcitrant (and resistance-creating) piston hanks. Some foils are designed with interlocking sections intended to speed the process of setting up standing rigging after launching or trailing, but this can prove more of a hin-drance than a help; and, in older variants, it seemed to exac-erbate the tendency for the sail to jam on hoisting or lowering.

Headsail furling gears are of course nothing new; the Wykeham Martin gear – simple in concept and operation with little more than a lower drum for the furling line and a swivel at the head of the sail – has been around for over half a cen-tury and was (and remains) a distinct improvement over tying in reef points on a plunging foredeck! The size of sail – or, more accurately, the length of the luff – was the limiting factor: until recently, cruising yachts favoured small headsails and were usually cutter as opposed to sloop rigged, setting not only staysail and jib, but frequently a jib topsail as well. It was not the custom to sail with standing rigging bar tight – indeed, skippers rarely perceived any need for doing so and, anyway, it is impossible with a sail set to the bowsprit end. Excess sag to leeward, though, which was more pronounced the longer the sail luff, meant that the furling was difficult to operate – so effectively ruling out Wykeham Martin gear for masthead Bermudan yachts. The contradictory twist of the luff wire and headsail sheet made it inadvisable to attempt windward work with the sail partially reduced in area, but with the line from the drum made fast, the reefed sail could be used safely enough downwind.

Occasionally, a heavy luff wire was employed in an effort to eliminate sag – which it did marginally, but the basic problem still remained. One other alternative was an internal light spar contained within a headsail luff sleeve; this functioned reasonably well – at least until the fabric stretched slightly about half-way through the season, leaving the spar to swivel, but the sail quite unmoved!

The basic principle of headsail furling gears has not altered; the sail is still reduced or furled by a line to a rotating drum, but today's technology has refined the equipment to the point where it can cope with the foresails of even the largest yacht. (Since the accent is now as much on the ability to attune headsail areas precisely to the wind velocity rather than simply furl or set them as required, these systems should perhaps more accurately be termed reefing gears.) The safest for the small yacht are, in my view, those that make use of the vessel's existing forestay (rather than replacing it with a solid extrusion) and that position over this an external freely rotating spar, grooved to accept the luff of the sail. This ensures that even if the spar is damaged, the forestay should remain intact.

Whatever type or make is fitted – and the best are examples of excellent engineering (complex, too, with removable drums for racing and twin grooves for alternating headsails) – attention must be paid not only to the bearings, but also upper and lower end fittings since the twisting force exerted during the reefing or furling process is considerable, even on a luff of 20 ft (6 m) or so. A jammed or poorly acting swivel could well damage the luff spar, leaving the sail well and truly jammed, and it will not furl (nor unfurl – the second corollary to Murphy's law dictating that whatever goes wrong will be that which places the vessel in the worst predicament!). Lowering the sail may also be out of the question, since twisting or bending of the luff spar could constrict the groove. In a chronic case, a binding or otherwise malfunctioning swivel will eventually injure the rigging or the terminals; should this happen at the masthead, it might escape notice until too late – though usually, difficulty in operating the gear would draw attention to the fact that all was not well before structural failure took place.

The possibility of the furling line breaking cannot be ignored, for it is subjected to a tremendous load during the reefing process. However, in spite of a theoretical awareness of this, many people persist in using undersized cordage (although, in some instances, the drum is not large enough for a rope of correct diameter). If the line (or cleat, for that matter) does carry away, the sail will break free with such violence that it may well be reduced to tatters before it can be brought under control.

What is practicable for the small yacht?

Once set up correctly, in practice there are relatively few failures of the gear per yacht per mile under way – but if one does occur, it can be pretty hair-raising. Probably, though, not many could compare to the experience of an acquaintance who, peaceably pursuing a course around Britain from west to east, was caught in a gale off the north coast of Scotland. Being an optimist by nature, he delayed reefing in the hope that the wind would go away if ignored, only to discover that (a) the wind continued to increase regardless, and (b) that the headsail reefing jammed and stubbornly refused to obey orders; this left him with no alternative but to sail widdershins down the coast until the weather eased (and by then he was off the Lizard and heading for Lowestoft the hard way!).

However, whether headsail reefing is actually worth having (or, for that matter, prudent) on a small sailing cruiser is open to doubt. It could be argued that with a working foresail area less than 100 sq ft (9.2 sq m) (and considerably less in many micro yachts), few crew members are going to experience much difficulty hauling home the sheets, albeit with the aid of winches. The ideal scenario of one sail for all wind strengths and directions is just that: an ideal scenario. The truth is rather different: in light winds, it will still be advantageous to set a genoa – perhaps downwind to fly a cruising chute or spinnaker; and in heavy going, the partially reefed headsail brings the centre of effort further forward than is desirable, and if the intention really is to cruise seriously and deal with

It is unusual to set a yawl rig on a yacht of less than 30 feet (9.1 m) in length, but the owner has managed it quite neatly on this 21 footer, with the aid of a jib set to a short bowsprit to balance the mizzen. The yawl is an excellent cruising rig, although the mizzen (abaft the rudder on a yawl, forward of it on a ketch) contributes little or nothing to the drive on the wind. However, good balance can be maintained when reducing sail – and the mizzen staysail is a very powerful reaching sail.

bad weather as it comes, a storm jib, set inboard from the stemhead, is a much better bet. This brings us to the matter of windage, for excess windage is even more detrimental to the behaviour of a small yacht than a larger craft simply because of the higher percentage in relation to overall length. This is more pronounced in the cruising boat because of the conflicting demands of accommodation space and headroom, which mean more freeboard and a higher superstructure, but it is also manifest in the spars and rigging. A headsail whose luff, for example, is 22 ft (6.7 m), will – when totally furled – become a tube with a diameter of about 3 in (7.6 cm): this amounts to an area of around 6 sq ft (0.5 sq m) (a little more than one-third of the average area of a small craft's storm jib). The extra windage from the furled sail doesn't sound much, but it is quite enough to deflect the boat to leeward when motoring or when motorsailing into the wind, with perhaps just a reefed mainsail set for steadying. If the yacht is in storm force conditions faced with lying a'hull or running under bare poles, the extra windage could be hazardous. True, the stowed mainsail presents a slightly larger area, but is concentrated lower and may in extremis be stowed on deck and a tri-sail set. If attempting to claw to windward under a reefed headsail and tri-sail, even the redundant furled headsail area will have a marked effect on leeway.

Headsail reefing systems are not by any means cheap either, though the cost may be hidden if included in the inventory of a new boat. However, if intending to fit gear to an older boat, it should be borne in mind that the outlay of £600–£1000 for the gear and headsail (at the time of writing) is unlikely to be recouped if the boat is later sold (although it might make it a more attractive proposition for a potential purchaser).

Depending upon condition and cloth weight, altering an existing sail so as to be compatible with the reefing system may not be out of the question; however, there are certain suppliers and manufacturers who adopt rather a high-handed attitude about this, refusing point blank to sell the gear without a custom sail as well. They do have a point, though, since the most efficient headsails are of specialised cut and construction.

Because the sail is subjected to hard use (even abuse), it must be of top quality so as to allow loads to be spread evenly whatever the area set. The sail has a tendency to increase in fullness as it is progressively reefed, and so a layer of high-density foam, shaped along the luff, is inserted to counteract this and to ensure that the sail stays flat. Bi- and tri-radial sail cutting helps to maintain the aerodynamic shape effectively throughout the broadest spectrum of wind strengths, and such a sail will be superior to one that is horizontally cut; this is not surprising, though it will be more expensive to produce. However, it really makes little sense to settle for second best.

As the furled sail will usually remain in situ for an entire season (sometimes for several), it should be safeguarded from its natural enemy: ultraviolet light. This degrades coloured Terylene sails very rapidly (darker shades such as tan and navy blue being the most susceptible), but white ones too will become brittle without a protective sacrificial strip of cloth sewn along the leech. This must be wide enough to encompass the entire sail when furled, but check that it is fixed to the correct side if the sail furls one way only (as some do). Each time the boat is left, ensure that the clew is secured and a tie passed around the sail so that it cannot possibly break adrift in a gale; nothing cheers the sailmakers' hearts more than the equinoxial crop of sails that have flogged themselves to death and have to be replaced!

Consider the cutter

So far as the small cruising vessel is concerned, there is much to recommend a rig with divided foretriangle – a cutter, strictly

Rigging a 'Poacher' cat ketch. The foresail and mainsail are each sleeved around the mast, encircled by the light wishbone boom. The masts are keel stepped and unstayed: they flex in stronger gusts, and so spill wind. Both sails need progressive reefing to achieve correct balance, though this can be carried out from the cockpit.

In heavy weather with only one sail set, manoeuvring with any degree of precision can be tricky, and balance (along with windward efficiency) will be impaired.

speaking, although the term now is pretty well interchangeable with the sloop that occasionally sets a storm jib on an inner forestay. This hybrid (known as the slutter) was common on both racing and cruising yacht of the 1950s and 1960s and has now reappeared in the guise of cutter or sloop depending upon a pedant's interpretation. Whatever the correct term, this is a sensible rig for the small boat so long as the inner forestay is clipped on to a pelican hook for easy removal (the stay then being brought back to the shrouds and clipped safely out of harm's way). Assuming this to be the case, a large headsail can be set for light weather or downwind sailing, since it will not foul the inner stay when coming about; in heavier going, the inner forestay can be set up and a small staysail (if of heavy cloth, this can double as a storm jib) can be used, perhaps in conjunction with a high-clewed jib for intermediate wind strengths. (The inner foresail can be rigged to be self-acting, either being set on a boom or fitted with a reinforced clew board; in either case, with sheets led to a horse or track, no attention is needed when tacking, and the sail is freed off in the normal manner for downwind work.)

As with all things, there are some drawbacks: if converting from sloop to cutter, care must be taken not to increase the working foresail area too, as this will result in lee helm – with the boat bearing away uncontrollably. There will inevitably be a slight increase in windage, though this will be less than would be associated with headsail reefing (especially reefing fitted to masthead sloop). The cost of the extra staysail, inner forestay, sheets, leads etc must also be taken into account, but even so, the option might well still prove more economical than the fitting of a conventional reefing system.

One oft-cited drawback to cutter rig is the need for running backstays, which seem, irrationally, to strike awe and terror into crews. Given a well-stayed masthead rig (single masthead forestay, two pairs of lower shrouds, one pair of cap shrouds, and standing backstay), there should be no need for runners on a small yacht – so long as the inner forestay is at the same height as the aft lowers and the inner staysail is in fact set to this. The case is altered, though, where there is a highly strung variant of fractional rig: here the standing rigging may be whittled down to the bare minimum with (if swept spreaders are employed) just a forestay, single pair of caps and in-line lower shrouds together with masthead backstay; with such a configuration, running backstays cannot be dispensed with. Yet in practice they are easy to set up – preferably, on a small yacht, with a simple downhaul to cam jamming cleats rather than the Highfield levers frequently still employed on larger craft. On the wind, there is no need to set up the weather stay and release the one to leeward; both can safely be left tensioned. Failure to adjust the runners off the wind, and particularly when sailing under spinnaker in fresh conditions, could conceivably result in the loss of the mast; but (look on the bright side) a cruising boat would probably not be thrashing along under such a press of sail while a racer would

A snappy little 16 footer. It is a remarkably pretty little boat – and at first glance appears much larger than it actually is – but this type of light and very beamy design must be sailed with the same care as a large dinghy or open keel boat. When at a steep angle of heel, the beam can be unsettling; to a nervous or inexperienced crew unsure of their footing, it would seem a very long drop into the water on the lee side!

have crew members detailed specifically to the task of setting up the runners!

Reefing the mainsail

Methods of reducing the mainsail area have not been neglected in the search for simpler sail handling – although, apart from the continual hazard of losing the reefing handle overboard, the now rather passé roller reefing, by which the foot of mainsail was wound around the boom, proved quite adequate for the majority of Bermudan rigged yachts: certainly it was easier to accomplish singlehanded and in a hurry than struggling to tie in a reef in a rising wind and sea. The set of the reefed sail always left something to be desired even in smaller craft, as the bulk of the material built up in the forward two-thirds of the boom; and unless the sail was cut so as to maintain the 90 degree angle desirable between mast and boom at all times (oddly enough, quite a rarity), the boom generally drooped at the outhaul. To counteract this, it was suggested that timber packing strips or 'whelps' were either glued to the after end of the boom – or carefully slipped into the leach of the sail as it was progressively rolled up (a fiddly operation, and surely yet another nugget of wisdom dating from the nostalgic era when all yachts carried paid hands!).

Slab reefing is now hailed as the answer to a sailor's prayers: so simple, so effortless, that it has become the norm – even though in reality it differs little from the traditional pendant and point system in use for countless generations. Several factors have contributed to this popularity, the first being that given the relatively short length of the boom in modern Bermudan rigs, it really does take only moments to haul down a section of sail so long as reefing lines and leads are correctly positioned, and it is quite possible to sail on cheerfully disregarding the swag of sailcloth flapping about the ears of the crew; to do so being looked upon more as a sign of insouciance rather than sloppiness on the part of the skipper! Far better, though, to secure the sail as nature intended: either by a lacing or by points (tied in under the boltrope if the mainsail has slides, or made fast with a reef knot under the boom). Leaving the surplus fabric slatting is distracting, causes chafe, and makes yet one more contribution to unwanted windage.

A certain amount of vertical flexion is considered to be worth having in the boom of a modern yacht (and vital in the case of a lightly sparred boat with fractional rig), and this, together with a degree of mast bend, permanent or induced, affects the draft of the sail, flattening it in stronger winds. In order to control the bend of the boom, the mainsheet will, instead of being attached at the extreme outer end, be positioned a third to half-way from aft, and may be fitted with an adjustable slide to alter the lead. The main will be sheeted for preference to a track of the maximum possible width with a traveller and control lines, rather than the old-fashioned and very imprecise system of a simple aft horse or eyebolts. Clearly, a centre mainsheet attachment is impracticable with a roller reefing sail, once a reef has been taken in; it is not impossible, though, as a claw ring can be used. The claw ring is quite effective so long as a limiter is rigged to prevent it sliding up and down the boom at will, and with a line from boom outhaul to mast, both mainsheet fitting and kicking strap can be set up with positions controlled from the cockpit. Apart from the cost (a good-quality claw is not cheap), there is little to its detriment – except that it can deal the unwary crew member an almighty clout on the head.

Simple enough as the slab method is in concept (at least there is no inaccessible mechanism to break), it does take a certain amount of practice to perfect the reefing operation, so make a few trial runs. As with a roller reefing headsail, the cut of the sail is crucial and so is cloth weight: it is a misconception that a lighter cloth not only improves the set of the mainsail, but makes reefing an easier operation; ideally, the sail should be fabricated from 5–6 oz (141–170 g) Terylene and, with cruising and general all-round use in mind, should be cut flat rather than full. Except for racing, the high-tech fabrics such as Mylar should not be considered; there is a slight gain in that the minimal distortion under load allows an optimum sail/spar match, but the material is not renowned for its user-friendly qualities and does not take kindly to careless handling or stowing. The additional cost, though, is rather less than might be expected; in the region of 30 to 40 per cent more than Terylene, and with the price differential becoming less marked with each passing year. In a small yacht with a dual role, the Mylar sails would really have to be backed up by a full cruising suit. Yet no matter which material is selected, there must be adequate reinforcement in way of the luff and leech cringles and, if ordering a new sail, it is worth giving some thought to just how much sail is reduced at one hit: often the first reef only takes out 20 per cent of the mainsail area, and in unsettled weather, a second reef might have to be pulled down hard on the heels of the first. With the mainsail of a small yacht, two reefs are really all that is practicable; if caught out in deteriorating conditions, it would be wise to lower the main, stow the boom on deck and, if progress has to be maintained to windward, set a storm tri-sail (without which no small cruiser should venture offshore).

Keep the complexities of the mainsail reefing pendants to a minimum; lines that can in theory be operated from the cockpit via turning blocks on deck may prove unreliable, as there is considerable loading on the pendants (even with a mainsail of 100 sq ft (9.2 sq m) in area), and achieving a fair lead to all controls takes a bit of management. In any case, so far as the micro yacht is concerned, the boom is light and the outhaul usually within the reach of the helmsman at all times.

Lazyjacks, which restrain the main during hoisting, lowering and reefing, are invaluable when sailing short-handed, and simple to rig from either single or twin topping lifts; not only do they take much of the fight out of a flogging sail, but

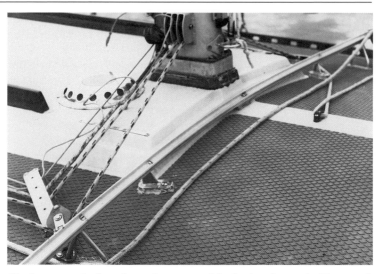

Heel exits to halyards with turning blocks leading aft. The track for the self-tacking foresail appears to be a later addition judging from the mastic smeared over and around the through-fastenings to the deck!

lazyjacks virtually make the mainsail self-stowing.

Fully battened mainsails have gained a following in both long-distance racing and cruising circles. These sails are extremely efficient square foot for square foot, since the battens support a heavy roach that in turn permits more of the sail area to be concentrated higher up – where it operates in clean air. For the cruiser, the accent is placed on the lack of flogging and the ease with which such a sail can be controlled during reefing and lowering – all these advantages are real enough, but the battens can briefly snag the mast when the sail is freed off or allowed to slat, thus catching partly aback. This causes difficulty in depowering the sail – possibly at a critical moment – when picking up a mooring or edging into a marina. This tendency (present, to a lesser degree, where there is a full-length top batten only) can also complicate hoisting and lowering, since the luff may jam in track or groove. To alleviate this, batten cars are used; but these create a gap, thus disrupting the smooth airflow between the sail and mast.

However, as with Chinese lug or junk rig, the full-length battens do ensure that the reefed or lowered sail, particularly when tamed by lazyjacks, drops neatly on to the boom – rather like a Venetian blind!

The Chinese lug

The Chinese lug – admittedly in a form somewhat more refined than in its native waters – has been offered as a viable cruising option on a number of production sailing craft ranging in size from ocean-voyaging 40 footers down to the Coromandel and Kingfisher 20 – both of which can be classified as micro yachts.

This rig evolved over many centuries and is perfect for its designed purposes, being easy to handle and adaptable to a wide range of conditions. Since junks were, as a rule, family concerns, run on the proverbial shoestring, the gear had to be obtained from local sources and to be cheap and simple to make. Cutting the sail was hardly a skilled operation, for the panels are flat and without flow, this being imparted by the sheetlets controlling the battens. The sail is easy to repair since external battens prevent flogging, and to prevent damage to one cloth spreading to its neighbour. The balance, though, depends to some extent on having two or three masts – and sails. A coasting or short-sea trading junk is a very different animal from an ocean-going yacht, above the waterline and below it, but the rig, generally adapted to ketch or schooner form, does seem to suit larger yachts very well: most of those who sail with it, swear by it.

On a small yacht with a single-masted configuration, the advantages are not so clear: the tapering unstayed mast is by its very nature expensive to build, whether it be of timber, aluminium or glassfibre. It is also comparatively heavy, and since it is stepped only just abaft the stem, unless the boat's forward waterline sections are quite full, it will cause the bow to undercut in a chop.

Admittedly, all sail handling can be carried out from the cockpit, eliminating the need for routine foredeck work, and very little physical effort is required to trim the sail. Few things could be less demanding than the act of reefing: the battens bring the sail down evenly and swiftly, and it is then only the work of moments to make everything secure. However, here's the drawback: the sail and battens are relatively heavy, and that reefed sail makes an unwieldy bundle at the foot. Windage is very considerable, and the pointing ability when reefed is quite noticeably impaired on a small boat. Downwind, the weight exacerbates the rolling moment to a marked degree – depending of course upon hull design and keel configuration.

One other minor niggle is the lack of sail in light winds; it is theoretically in order to set a ghoster or genoa flying, but care should be exercised – bearing in mind the chance of over-stressing the mast: any such sail should be set on a sacrificial halyard (ensure, though, that there's a line made fast to both halyard and the head of the sail; losing either should the halyard fail-safe and break as designed would be highly embarrassing). Unfortunately, since one of the strongest points in favour of the junk rig is that only the single balanced lug mainsail is needed for all winds, hanging up any other canvas could be taken as an admission of defeat! (On the grounds of economics too, the junk rig is claimed to compare favourably with the conventional sloop, with the fact that sail and mast are fractionally dearer being outweighed by dispensing with sail tracks, winches and ancillary sails!)

There is not enough space here to detail all the many fascinating alternative rigs. Some ideas are excellent in concept, but complicated to set up initially; some are of dubious practical value; and some should never have been offered for public consumption until the wrinkles had been ironed out. Many of the self-acting rigs suffer from the drawbacks of the Chinese lug – namely, excess windage when reefed and the irritating inability to set light-weather sails with any degree of confidence. In certain types, it is also difficult – if not actually impossible – to maintain the boat's balance once the sail area is reduced, even in some of the light twin-masted designs. To be honest, in a number of cases this is at least partly due to the rig being unsuited to the hull configuration (usually one with a combination of deep narrow fin and lack of forefoot). At worst, the boat can be unresponsive to the helm – declining to come about or holding any semblance of the desired course. It is easy to be dismissive of these innovative rigs, but in some conditions the wishbone cat ketch, in particular, excels; although not pointing as high as it might, it can give an exhilarating ride in up to Force 6 or so – even running by the lee with no fear of gybing. The flexible masts should spill wind and thus adjust to the prevailing strength, but this is rather optimistic and it will prove necessary to reef both main and foresail progressively. If sailing to windward, the first tuck will probably be taken at the upper end of Force 4 – about 15 knots. Much beyond 22 knots, however, and sail area has to be reduced more drastically – which means dropping one sail, thereby ruining the balance; it is then difficult in the extreme to hold the boat on course and the combined windage of both reefed and stowed sails precludes any serious attempt at making up to windward. If there is a moral, it is to sail such a boat in as wide a variety of wind strengths before making any commitment to purchase.

A Coromandel with a modern version of junk rig (Chinese lug) at hull speed in a force 7. Although the yard and battens are light in weight, on a dead run they are enough to exacerbate any tendency to roll. When reduced in area too, there is quite an unwieldy bundle at the foot.

A return to gaff?

Going from one extreme to the other, from the frankly unorthodox to the traditional, gaff rig is making quite a comeback; however, perhaps it would really be fairer to say that small gaff-rigged yachts of classic appearance are enjoying a revival. The majority of these little craft, however, being built in GRP or epoxy-encapsulated timber, are thus unlikely to suffer the classic structural problems of their forebears! By the same token, the updated gaff cutter or sloop rig as used on these designs is aimed at being trouble-free in so far as handling and maintenance are concerned. Gaff rig as seen on working smacks in all its baggywrinkled, deadeyed and lanyarded splendour, with jib and jackyard topsails, acres of mainsail and watersails festooned beneath boom and bowsprit, is a sight to gladden the heart – but perhaps the heart of the onlooker rather than those on board, for the winches are looked upon as effete and decadent on such craft!

Gaff rig has now undergone a subtle process of alteration aimed at bringing it into line with the perceived requirements of the family crew: although still with a relatively large main-to-foretriangle ratio, the disparity has been reduced and the mast is now generally stepped a little further aft – making it possible to shorten boom and gaff slightly with a consequent reduction in weight. As modern yachts are, on the whole, lighter and more easily driven than their counterparts of yesteryear, the total working sail area can be reduced without any detriment to performance in moderate wind strengths. This certainly makes it easier to relax and enjoy the sailing – whether pottering under main and working headsail, or nailing up everything bar the dishcloths in best 'old gaffer' fashion. The rig's large main generates considerable power on a reach, and this is very noticeable – whereas the slight loss of the windward edge might not be. Though always dogged by a propensity to roll ponderously on a dead run – exacerbated by the weight of boom and gaff – this is much diminished by today's lighter spars. Those who become fascinated with the rig (and many do) will soon learn all the tricks of tricing up or scandalising the mainsail, and to handle the sails as used to be the custom before the coming of the 'iron topsail'!

4 The Integrity of the Rig

Whether the rig is simple or complex, Bermudan or gaff cutter, set up for cruising or tensioned to screaming pitch, it will all count for nothing if it is either badly designed or if spars and standing rigging are of indifferent quality or badly maintained. Nowhere is the old adage about the lack of a horseshoe nail demonstrated more aptly than with the standing rigging of a yacht, and its literal truth will be obvious to anyone troubling to examine the rigging of a random sample of boats, large or small. It doesn't matter if the wire is over spec or terminals and rigging screws are the best available, for whether the mast remains upright or descends abruptly to deck level ultimately depends upon the small split rings or pins in the clevis pins. The interested observer examining these random boats will see pins that have not been opened out, rusted, broken or missing. Shroud rollers, protective gaiters on bottlescrews (to say nothing of plastic-taped mummy wrappings), may hide a potentially hazardous state of affairs, so don't risk sailing a new boat without checking very thoroughly indeed – not only at deck level, but also at masthead and hounds fittings. Although it is common practice to tape or otherwise cover rigging screws and terminals, it is unnecessary; furthermore, it traps dirt and damp and prevents regular inspection. Inspection should be routine; apart from damage and deterioration, it is not unknown for vandals and malicious practical jokers to target rigging if the boat is accessible – I have known several cases including one where each and every split pin was removed from the deck fittings of a 30 ft (9.1 m) ketch lying alongside in a marina berth. The tape was then replaced, and the sabotage only came to light in the course of a survey. Luckily this vessel never put to sea before the deficiency was discovered, but boats can and do sail around with one or two pins damaged or absent, with the skippers blissfully unaware of the fact. The mast may remain intact, with the clevis pins retained in place by the stress on shrouds or stays; but given weather or a sea state that sets up vibration in the rig, the outcome would be less happy.

Before dealing in more detail with the standing rigging, it would be a good idea to consider the mast, since the type and material, and also the way in which it is stepped, determines the type of standing rigging upon which its existence depends!

The mast and spars

In the absence of any other suitable material, masts for small craft were invariably made of timber and could be subdivided into two types: weighty, massive in section and solid, often of pitch pine, as found on heavy displacement cruisers and working craft; or light (verging on delicate) and hollow, constructed of laminated spruce – and found on racing boats. There were compromises, especially with bespoke cruising boats, but the general pattern was well established until the generation of small and light 'pocket cruisers' of the 1950s and 1960s. With sailing increasing in popularity, far more attention was paid to simultaneously bettering performance under sail and keeping all the costs of mass production to an acceptable commercial minimum. The introduction of the aluminium mast obligingly fulfilled both of these criteria, with simple extrusions proving – after initial experiments with sections and wall thickness – to be strong, offering a considerable saving in weight aloft, a slightly lower centre of gravity and, so long as the mast was of constant diameter (a forgone conclusion in the masthead rig universally adopted) from truck to heel, very economical to produce. And as if these qualities were not in themselves sufficient to ensure a unanimous overnight switch from wood to metal, spars were also claimed to be maintenance free; yet the early masts, which were rarely anodised, developed surface corrosion after a few seasons' exposure to salt air, and this – although not prejudicial to strength – was unsightly. The anodising process that was later adopted gave a smooth, highly finished surface that needed only a fresh water wash at the end of each season (although of course all fittings, whether stainless steel or cast aluminium alloy, required normal routine inspection and overhaul).

Very few production racing or cruising small yachts – with the exception of the classic variants such as the Skanner, Cornish Shrimper or Winkle Brig – are now offered with timber spars as standard. Aluminium is pretty well universally regarded as being far superior. There are dissident voices, though, and these draw attention to the possibility of metal fatigue. This appears to take place gradually over a period of years and is thought to result from the pitch of the vibration of a highly tensioned rig. Also, the practice of leaving the mast stepped year in year out, with rigging tensioned as though for competition, with nary a respite even when the boat is laid up ashore, must exacerbate the process.

The onset of fatigue is unlikely to be spotted; the protective anodising applied to the surface (generally of pure aluminium

Dismasting! This photo was taken in a gust of around 40 knots in the Solent that claimed several victims when shrouds or swages parted.

or aluminium oxide) is thin in the extreme, but might possibly show minute surface anomalies, a definite warning sign of incipient problems in the underlying alloy. Compression stress, on the other hand, whether resulting simply from failure of a lower shroud, inner forestay or running backstay (or, on a highly tuned boat, possibly occurring as a result of uneven rig tensioning), should be visible as a series of transverse wrinkles. A look along the length of the luff groove is worthwhile too, for any localised constriction suggests that the mast has been stressed and can no longer be trusted.

One of the most common causes of dismasting – apart from the practice of opting for the slimmest possible section to minimise weight and windage aloft – is breakage of the fittings. Once again, fatigue is often the culprit: fatigue engendered by constant slight flexing of the tangs over a period of years. Even where the mast is of appropriate section for the boat, fittings may still err on the light side and, as always, require checking on a regular basis. Where the fittings themselves are strong, rivets may become corroded or tired – and this at least is easy enough to spot before serious trouble occurs.

Although often listed as an inducement to those purchasing a second-hand yacht ('original spruce mast' etc), not many owners would actually go to the length of swapping the alloy spars for timber; this would in any case prove impractical in the case of some of the modern highly stressed fractional rigs.

Care of a wooden mast

A wooden spar needs care and attention; on the other hand, once varnished to perfection, it looks marvellous. Arguably, it is this constant maintenance (that tends to be so neglected in metal spars) that contributes to the low failure rate, but of course fail they do from time to time. However, assuming the mast or boom is of correct size for the yacht and of first-quality clear timber, it is unusual for a cruising yacht's spars to be lost as a direct result of any structural breakdown of the actual timber. However, the mast of a cruiser will usually be solid, possibly laminated from two, sometimes three, scarphed lengths of timber, whereas a racing boat will opt for the slightly lighter hollow type (often with a luff groove rather than an external track) and the tolerances may be miscalculated. Certainly with a hollow spar, failure in the glue line or shakes (splits along the length of the grain) will rapidly affect the integrity; and if left untreated, they will ensure the downfall of the mast!

In the case of delamination, no matter whether the spar is solid or hollow in section, it will be necessary to take a saw and open the affected part of the glue line before relaminating with resorcinol or epoxy resin.

Shakes, so long as they are not too extensive, can be filled and then varnished to prevent water penetration and subsequent rot, but those of more than 1/4 in (6 mm) in depth may require the insertion of a sliver of timber and then glueing; really deep shakes, especially if several occur in the same locality, mean that the mast should be condemned. Far more serious (in fact, usually fatal to the spar in question) are the tiny cracks across the grain that indicate compression stress. These are difficult to spot, but a slight wrinkling of the varnish may give them away. If the mast is in any way bent along its length (or 'sprung'), take a magnifying glass and peer suspiciously at the timber in way of the hounds fitting (the attachment point of the lower shrouds).

If the mast (or boom) has an external track for the mainsail, ensure that all lengths are securely fastened and free from protruding screw heads that will cause the slides to jam; for the same reason, ensure that joins in the track butt as closely as possible. Where a luff groove is used instead of track (not common on the dedicated cruiser), there is always the possibility of rot in the section of spar inside the groove, so this area should be protected with several coats of thinned varnish. Usually, the lower end is protected against the possibility of injury from the sail's headboard by a hardwood edging;

Rigging

1 The head of an aluminium mast showing the crane for the backstay (which carries the sail clear of the mast-head) and the tangs to the forestay and cap shrouds. These might be fabricated of stainless steel or of cast aluminium alloy. Hard eyes in the rigging wire are formed by Talurit splices and the connection to tangs and crane is by means of rigging links.

2 The hounds fitting of a typical modern aluminium mast with 'T' pieces or button terminals roller-swaged on to the lower shrouds (in this sketch there is a swageless terminal on the three quarter height forestay). These simply slot into the spar and are held in place by the tension of the rig.

3 A swageless terminal. The fitting is screwed over the wire and an internal cone or wedge of a softer metal. The end result is very strong, indeed it is claimed to be as strong as the wire itself, and fitting is within the capabilities of the amateur. Since the terminal does not require specialised equipment, rigging can be carried out with the mast stepped to ensure perfect accuracy. For this reason too, swageless terminals, and extra wire, are worth carrying for emergency use.

4 A spider band of steel or wrought iron. These are in common use on older traditional timber masts. The crane carries the jib halyard clear of the inner staysail halyard. The standing rigging, which would frequently be of galvanised flexible wire, has a soft eye without a thimble, the wire being joined by a hand splice, parcelled and served.

5 Often in older boats, the shrouds are simply slipped over timber chocks. The method seems rather haphazard but works well in practice. However, the chocks must be examined every year for evidence of any rot or movement. The standing rigging would use soft eyes and, as shown here, Talurit swages (or possibly, hand splices).

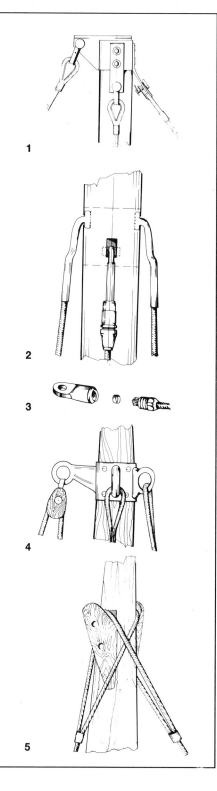

1

2

3

4

5

unfortunately, this is not normally carried higher than 6 in (15 cm) or so, and the softwood edges easily become eroded or split to such an extent that the sail may pull free of the groove when under load.

Once it was general practice to step each and every mast through the deck, and directly on to the backbone of the vessel, with the downthrust being transmitted directly to the hog with the stress at deck level distributed by knees and the beefed-up beams known as the mast partners (with bulkheads and integrally moulded internal stiffening being substituted in GRP craft). In older timber boats, there was a measurable amount of play at deck level, with the mast being finally positioned – and the rake adjusted – by slender wedges hammered into place as required. Traditionally, watertight integrity depended upon a canvas lagging heavily coated with paint and tacked both to mast and deck; despite this, weeps were inevitable. Nowadays, however, the use of neoprene gaiters, tightened down with worm drive hose clips, has all but removed that particular aggravation. For a seagoing cruiser, the keel-stepped mast possesses one marked advantage over a deck-stepped one: should the standing rigging fail, there is a better than even chance that at least part of the spar will remain standing and so make it simpler to set a jury rig. Depending upon which stay or shroud does part, a deck-stepped mast often goes clear over the side; if it does not immediately sink, given a fairly calm sea state, it *might* be possible for a light spar to be restepped by the crew once the rigging is repaired – but this would be out of the question with the mast of a 30 footer. By rigging a parbuckle, it might be feasible to haul the spar on board, but putting it back where it belongs would be physically impossible except with outside assistance. However, even in a small yacht, any prospect of restepping the mast would be totally ruled out if the incident occurred in heavy weather (the most likely scenario), since there would be a strong possibility that it would have to be cut free in order to avoid damaging the hull.

Of course, in a vessel of 30 ft (9.1 m) or so, even a deck-stepped mast would need to be raised or lowered with the aid of a crane or at least a sheerlegs, whereas the mast of the average micro cruiser can be set up with ease by a couple of crew members; indeed, this can usually be managed singlehanded with an A-frame and hingeing heel step or tabernacle.

Stepping the mast on deck may increase the amount of usable accommodation space slightly, since with the loading distributed to bulkheads or twin pillars, there will be an unobstructed area amidships; perhaps here too the dictates of comfort below take precedence over demands of seaworthiness: in this case, dismasting – which naturally only happens to other people!

Alterations to the rig

When buying a yacht, it is usually taken for granted that the rig is more or less as the designer originally intended, but passing trends – and owners who modify the yachts to conform to these – can wreak havoc on the yacht's balance (and the structure too), yet these alterations may not be immediately apparent.

The first step along the scheduled path of improvements is usually from keel- to deck-stepped mast, generally with the aim of reducing the time and energy needed to raise and lower the spar. Also, reducing the length by 4 ft (1.2 m) or so might effect a very slight reduction in the overall cost. Such alteration is fine as far as it goes, but it is wise to ascertain that structural modifications have also been carried out – and not only with regard to the fitting of heel plate or tabernacle. If buying the boat, check for possible indications of compression stress; with a GRP yacht, these would include hairline crazes radiating from the mast heel and associated craze lines at the lower edge of the coachroof; in the case of a vessel of classic construction, poorly fitting knees and movement of deck beams may be a clear indication that additional strengthening is needed. Whatever the method of build (including marine ply or moulded veneer), be on the lookout for a hollowing of the coachroof or deck profile in the vicinity of the heel fitting.

Bowsprits and bumpkins may be tacked on freely, and indeed frequently are. Unless an owner has been unduly optimistic and has aimed at recreating either a racing smack (with a bowsprit accounting for about half of the overall length) or taken a fancy to a yawl rig (in which case, a bumpkin may be needed to sheet home the mizzen), there is not a lot of justification for either extension in a small yacht – though they are seen from time to time. Where someone has got it into their head to transmute a conventional sloop or cutter into a junk – let alone one of the other deviant rigs – the buyer should be wary. Granted, little more than a knowledge of hull and rig design is needed along with a certain amount of common sense, but regrettably these qualities are too often allied to misplaced optimism! Also, a proportion of those who go in for such drastic amendments to the yacht's original concept tend to be on a tight budget, so the specification of spars and sail may not be of the highest quality. This being the case, examine the mast, note the diameters and all other relevant measurements, and if anything looks doubtful, consult one of the companies with a specialised knowledge of such a rig. Then sail the boat, for the trim of a micro yacht has a marked sensitivity to weight and may be most unhappy with the mast stepped so far forward. The centre of effort of the rig will be critical too; and with only a single sail, the consequences of a miscalculation will be costly (perhaps even impossible) to rectify.

Gaff and Bermudan rig seem to change places depending on individual whim, the results generally being workable, although sometimes poorly suited to the character of the yacht. Much the same is true of masthead and fractional Bermudan sloops, with some long-suffering craft being revamped several times. The primary risk is that running backstays, diamonds and bracer stays were merrily consigned to the scrap heap on conversion to masthead rig – except, by the pessimistic (although not necessarily misguided) belt-and-braces brigade – but never a thought spared for the dimensions of the mast. This, even though cocooned by standing rigging, still has to be of heavier section if masthead rigged. While it is possible to strengthen the upper section of a wooden mast, this is ruled out with an alloy spar, which is cut and welded to achieve the desired taper above the hounds. That some yachts do undergo great sufferings in the cause of keeping up with current fashion trends in rigs is borne out by a little Blackwater sloop I knew well: originally built just after the last war and launched as a three-quarter-rigged stemhead sloop with brace, running backstays and single standing backstay with bumpkin, it first metamorphosed into a masthead sloop (still with runners) then to a three-quarter-rigged cutter – at which stage in the lifecycle it grew a long bowsprit (but ill-advisedly lost the running backstays and brace just when it needed them most). When last seen, sailing purposefully onwards, the bowsprit had gone (so had the bumpkin, which meant that the mainsail would no longer clear the standing backstay on coming about) and it had become a masthead cutter!

Rigging wire and terminals

With the exception of unstayed rigs where the spars are specifically designed to flex, the mast relies upon standing rigging to counteract the forces imposed upon it by the sails (and, to a lesser extent, by its own weight and windage). Essentially a

The stark but efficient layout on the deck of the Red Fox. All sail controls lead aft to the cockpit, as do the tackles for lifting the bilge boards.

mast is a strut in compression and so is dependent upon each shroud and stay to maintain this status quo; should one component fail for any reason, the mast will collapse, snapping off at the point of maximum stress or proceeding smartly over the side – though, in the latter case, with a chance that it may remain intact.

Although the rigger may have a degree of leeway in so far as the small- to medium-sized cruiser is concerned, stresses in the competitive yacht must be calculated with mathematical accuracy as the dimensions of mast and standing rigging will be of the minimum size allowable. Because there is only a hairline separating a rig of optimum aerodynamic form and one that folds in on itself like a trombone at the first squall, spar manufacturer and rigger must co-operate closely with each other – and with the designer.

Both those who race at club level (as opposed to the international circuit) and those who scorn what to them is mindless rounding of buoys to the accompaniment of swearing and shredding sails, sometimes appear to take a relaxed attitude to the rigging of their boat and are remarkably disinclined to question either the wire gauge, breaking strain – or, for that matter, the strength and condition of the terminals and rigging screws and deck fittings with which the whole affair is set up!

There is of course no doubt about it: the heavier the wire, the stronger it will be, but the more windage it will create. Wind resistance being one of the evils that dog the small yacht, this is obviously best kept to the minimum level compatible with safety (there should be allowed at least a further 30 per cent increment in size to allow for manufacturing flaws or unforeseen conditions). The breaking strain of the wire depends not only upon the gauge, but also on whether it is of galvanised or stainless steel, and also upon the manner of lay: the condition is also of paramount importance. Apart from single-strand piano wire – used occasionally on bracer stays, but otherwise only suitable for the standing rigging of dinghies and the very smallest yachts – most craft now rely upon stainless steel wire rope for the standing rigging, and often this is also used for certain halyards – running backstays too, where these are fitted. In newer boats, those that have yet to suffer the attentions of enthusiastic amateur re-riggers, the wire of shrouds and stays is normally of the type known as 1 by 19. This describes the way in which the wire is formed: a single strand at the heart and external wires (19 in number) surrounding it, and together forming a resilient yet fairly stiff wire. It is in fact rather too stiff to be run through blocks or sheaves; and so for halyards or other running rigging a more flexible type of rope is required – that most commonly in use being known as 7 by 7. As the term suggests, here there are seven strands, each made up of seven finer filaments of wire, sometimes laid up around a rope core. This wire can be either of galvanised or stainless steel and, as well as being spliceable by hand, can also be Talurit swaged, even in the larger diameters where this is not recommended for 1 by 19 wire. Talurit swaging, the simplest and cheapest, offers a means of joining two wires by applying great force to a soft metal collar; this method is widely employed on small craft.

Normally the cap shrouds and outer forestay of a small yacht would not be in excess of 1/5 in (5 mm) (with the standing backstay, lowers and inner forestay possibly made up of 4 mm), and even this might be thought by some to err on the side of caution. Since few craft of this type are likely to use wire over this diameter, the limitation of Talurits should not apply; however, it is worth pointing out that this type of swage should not be used to form hard eyes on 1 by 19 wire over 5 mm as the wire becomes overstressed, separating the strands when it is forced into taking up a sharp curve over the thimble.

Alternatives to this type of swaging are either external roller swaging or swageless terminals (where the wire is actually compressed over a soft metal cone). One point in favour of the latter method is that the rigging can be safely made up by an amateur – albeit a confident and careful one – with only the aid of ordinary hand tools. Both of these systems incorporate the terminals: fork, eye or entire rigging screw at the lower end and usually a 'button' or T-piece for use with the appropriate mast fitment. When rerigging, an anomalous situation sometimes comes about where the heavier wire is employed: if the mast fittings will not accept standard terminals – and older ones will not have been designed to do so – in spite of the integrity of the lower terminals, there will be no alternative to Talurit swaging hard eyes with rigging links to the fitting on the mast, thereby cancelling out half the advantage gained from the high-spec lower terminals! Neither roller swaging nor swageless terminals are suitable for use with every kind of wire, so check with the manufacturers first of all – especially before purchasing wire by the reel (as club members jointly might do).

Stainless steel and galvanised steel wire weigh the same, foot for foot, though in both cases the 1 by 19 lay is rather heavier than the flexible equivalent, 7 by 7. It now all becomes complicated: while the nominal breaking load of stainless and galvanised is identical in the 1 by 19 (3000 lb (1361 kg) in the case of 4 mm wire), where the wire is 7 by 7, the galvanised possesses greater strength than the stainless steel (2500 lb (1134 kg) as opposed to 2150 lb (975 kg) for 4 mm wire). Other flexible wire lays such as 7 by 12 and 7 by 19 vary slightly in strength relative to the more commonly used 7 by 7.

If buying wire in any sort of quantity, the cost differential between wire types is not all that great either, so why is stainless steel so universally popular? Well, it is more durable – or, perhaps it would be fairer to say that it lasts for longer without obvious corrosion or weakness. As soon as the galvanising wears off (which seems to happen within the space of months rather than years), surface rust forms on ordinary steel, so the metal must be given a regular protective coating of boiled linseed oil. This greatly extends the lifespan, but does of course mark sails (or anything else with which it comes into contact). One solution is to fit shroud rollers but, as these tend to become water traps, they will increase the rate of corrosion. Galvanised wire should not be expected to last for ever, nor of course should stainless. And to some extent the very absence of discernible corrosion can lead to the mistaken belief that the stainless wire remains sound for the lifespan of the yacht, but if it does part (which eventually it may, though possibly as a result of fatigue due to continuous flexing rather than corrosion), it nearly always goes without prior warning. Since it snaps with a great deal of force and the parted ends immediately fan out, it can inflict a very nasty injury. At least the corrosion, and occasionally 'soldiers' and broken strands in galvanised wire, gives some indication of incipient breakdown.

In the majority of cases of rigging failure, it may be the terminals, rigging screws or links that are to blame. Close inspection of all these may pre-empt trouble (occasionally a hairline fatigue crack may be seen in the shoulders of a fork or deck eye), but generally deterioration takes place unseen and unsuspected (or is in-built, the result of faulty forging or welding). It is possible to conduct a non-destructive test on the terminals by means of electronic resistance comparison, claimed to be capable of detecting internal corrosion, broken wire strands, defective swaging (and movement within a swage) and also cracked terminals. As with the majority of tests, it does not offer a guarantee that future problems will not occur, but it could be considered as an alternative to regular replacement of the rigging.

The human factor

However, it is the human factor most frequently at the root of all troubles. Rigging screws with forks unfair to the deck eyes are far from unusual, and place considerable strain on the terminal and the wire, especially on lower shrouds and inner forestay; toggles should always be used in order to provide a better lead to the wire and to function as a universal joint.

The standing rigging should have been initially cut exactly

If there is an opportunity, always have a last-minute check around the boat before singling up lines and casting off from the pontoon.

to the necessary length (odd links of chain or supernumerary shackles are clumsy and look unsightly, but far worse is a rigging screw opened out to danger point). I personally am unhappy if there is not 3/4 in (19 mm) of thread within the barrel at both ends; others are more sanguine and suggest a minimum of five turns. Obviously the rigging screw must be prevented from turning under load. Often, though, it will be apparent when looking at rigging that one or both of the locking nuts on the bottlescrews are missing and that no attempt has been made to mouse the fitting with wire.

Yet despite the commonplace defects in split pins and rings (and the absence of them altogether) in spite of their all-important role, and the fact that a situation that exists on deck may be duplicated at the masthead, the attachment of standing rigging to mast and deck fittings seems to be treated with surprising nonchalance. Shackles, even though never really meant as substitutes for links or clevis pins, do no real harm so long as they are secured with a wire mousing and are of appropriate size – but so often the tiny stainless steel strip shackles, intended only for a dinghy, are pressed into service; or going to the other extreme, 4 mm wire is married to massive (and generally rusted) galvanised examples that would not look out of place on a Thames barge! Even snap shackles are used on occasion, and this really is a practice to be deplored since they are liable to spring open under load. Although modern variants are claimed to be immune to this, I am by nature a doubter and would only entrust the mast to one as a short-term emergency measure – and only if there was no other alternative whatsoever. I hesitate even to use snap shackles on halyards for the same reason – halyard and sail parting company at the wrong moment is no laughing matter, and might even endanger the boat. Indeed, to prevent such a mishap, there should ideally be a light line from the head thimble to deck, which can do double duty in preventing the halyard soaring up to the masthead if a shackle parts (or if the cringle tears out of the sail – which does happen, though luckily not too often), and can also be used as a downhaul if the sail or halyard jams.

Anything breaking, snarling up or coming adrift at the mast truck can be the very devil to sort out on a small yacht. Admittedly, being forced to lower the mast on land or when anchored in sheltered waters is a nuisance and time-consuming, but it is hardly a major feat. At sea, though, it might be a different story, and the operation would carry with it an appreciable risk of damaging the spar if anything got out of control. The alternative, going aloft, is no easy task on a very small yacht – even assuming that one of the crew is willing and able to do so, and that there is another available to haul and tail the halyard. For one thing, it must be remembered that the mast will be a light, relatively fragile structure and will whip above the hounds – conceivably to danger point. And once above spreader height, the crew's own weight will induce a vicious pendulum roll that will gain momentum, thereby making it awkward to work – and so, possibly, induce more complications (including that of having the person aloft lose their nerve and freeze!). Few crews of small craft seriously contemplate the possibility of trouble above deck level, and so active efforts to avoid it are rare; but the provision of a spare halyard (ensure that there is a topping lift even when there is also a rigid kicker strut) and a downhaul to each halyard should help avoid the need for climbing expeditions. It is never a good idea to coerce a reluctant or inexperienced person into going aloft; and don't ever rely upon a sling made up of only a single rope, as this will quickly cut off the circulation to the hindquarters – which is nowhere near as amusing as it sounds!

In most instances, what applies to a modern boat with aluminium spars and Bermudan rig also goes for the older yacht

A well-made and comfort-
able bosun's chair makes a
great deal of difference
when going aloft, but this
can still be quite a lively
undertaking given the
movement of a small yacht.
Prevention is better than
cure: all masthead and
hounds fittings must be
carefully checked at the
start of each season, split
pins replaced and opened
out, and shackles that
might vibrate loose should
be moused with wire. There
ought to be at least one
spare halyard rove, and a
line from each halyard eye
ensures that it will not disappear irretrievably if the
shackle to the sail does fail.
    Although the halyards of
a small yacht – assuming
they are in a sound state –
will be up to an adult's
weight, external blocks
may not be, so take care. In
this photo, the footwear,
arguably, is less than ideal
– flexible shoes are best;
never go aloft with bare
feet.

with a timber mast and boom; there may, however, be some
discrepancies in the rigging of vintage yachts. Except for sail
and gooseneck tracks, just about every fitting will probably be
attached via hard eyes and shackles to one or more spider
bands, forged steel or iron collars, each one with perhaps as
many as half-a-dozen eyes on to which are shackled stays and
halyard blocks.
    Although even these basic blacksmith's fabrications can fail
– usually due to corrosion, fatigue or wear on the lower parts
of the forged eyes, as with galvanised steel wire – such fittings,
of heavy and agricultural appearance though they are, do
show signs of giving up the ghost before actually doing so.
Wear on the eyes is easily visible and, if there is surface corrosion, running fine sandpaper over the metal may reveal the

development of telltale cracks. As an alternative to mast bands, the standing rigging may simply have soft eyes (ie loops formed without thimbles) and these are dropped over angled wooden chocks fixed to the mast. By modern standards, this looks very unsophisticated, but as long as the chocks are sound with no splits or rot, the method is perfectly acceptable since everything is held in place by the tension of the rig – and so long as nothing breaks, there it will stay! In essence, the principle is identical to the internal button or 'T' terminals that slot into mast eyes on a modern rig.

Problems with hardware

At the root of a number of troubles are the chain plates and deck eyes to which the lower parts of the standing rigging are attached. The external strap chain plates – those associated mainly with wooden yachts and a few of the earliest GRP small craft – rarely give cause for concern; the loading of the rig is indirect and well distributed with an ample margin of strength in both fastenings and metal straps. Even when, on grounds of appearance and improving the headsail sheeting angles on beamy boats, it became the norm to fit chain plates internally instead of externally, apart from the odd weep where the fittings passed through the deck, major problems were unusual and could be spotted before becoming a serious threat. Yet with deck eye plates, now pretty well universal on GRP yachts at least, came a whole new era of problems, not least of which is structural damage to the deck itself.

Deck eyes carrying shrouds and/or forestay are of course subjected to what is virtually a direct upwards pull, only slightly lessened when the boat heels. Since this is so transparently obvious, it is hard to credit that in numerous instances there is no other provision for distributing the loading: the eyes are bolted through the GRP sandwich of the deck – occasionally through timber decking (in this case, eyes are almost invariably a later substitution aimed at 'modernising' a wooden yacht) – and it is by no means unknown for these fittings to be fixed without so much as a backing plate! Although one or two heavily laid-up early glassfibre yachts avoided problems by bolting through a laminate massively reinforced at the deck edge, a worrying number of smaller production yachts (and far too many larger ones) show signs of strain around the eyes after just a few seasons. Often, a straightedge laid across the deck will show that the glassfibre surrounding the fitting is starting to lift, and from this point onwards matters can only deteriorate: the sidedeck will rapidly delaminate as a result of water penetration (eventually splitting right from gunwale to coachroof side), and there is a strong possibility that the eye plate will pull free with consequent loss of the rig. Sometimes the telltale signs are not spotted in time, or the significance of them is underestimated. The deck eyes should always be internally backed up, either by a steel strap taken to a bulkhead or strong point internally. This is a point to watch for in cases where an inner forestay has been added – often this lacks internal reinforcement: the fitting should be taken to a bulkhead or the forepart of the coachroof. Another option is to carry a strop with bottlescrew tensioner to a further eye plate bolted to a flange on the keel – the wire can be removed in harbour, leaving the forward berths unobstructed. Unfortunately, in order to check on just how well the loading of the shroud eye is distributed, the headlining will probably have to be taken down. Like so many things on board a yacht, this is far easier said than done: a factory-fitted headlining, unless specifically provided with removable panels, is frustratingly tricky to replace. Nevertheless, if intending to cruise offshore, an inspection should be made – if only for peace of mind. If there is crazing in way of the eye plates, that inspection should not be delayed for long.

The forestay fitting is as a rule incorporated in the stemhead fitting, along with bow roller. It is probably true to say that it is the strongest fitting on board a small yacht, and one that is well suited to the loading demanded of it. At least, it starts out that way, but as it is also arguably the fitting most susceptible to impact, any signs of movement or repair justify a second look at the fastenings – which may have been sheared or wrenched. If the forestay is set inboard from the stem, it is an idea to ascertain that there is indeed internal reinforcement and bracing. About the only item of standing rigging that doesn't give rise to concern in the normal way of things is the backstay – or it was until the craze for using twins on a span and tensioning the whole affair over and above the call of duty! This can cause movement in the case of strap chain plates as the force pulls the upper edges towards one another.

Admittedly, many small yachts are hardly longer overall than many a cruising (or racing) dinghy, but will be considerably heavier – especially when equipped for passage making. Almost without exception, the micro yacht will also be more stable and so impose far greater loading on the rig. It is therefore quite worrying to see standing rigging and deck equipment similar in type and dimension to that encountered in an open boat of similar length; but time and again this proves to be the case. If in doubt, check breaking loads of all wire and consult with the manufacturers of the terminals and all associated fittings: this is far less trouble than losing a mast or damaging the deck or coachroof!

5 Theory and Practice

W hether the art of sailing is acquired by pottering around with family or friends, comes from hard-earned experience, or is formally taught in training sessions ashore and afloat, just about everyone is aware – in theory, at any rate – of the way in which the sails of a yacht convert the wind into a driving force. Once learned, this information is never quite forgotten, though most of us, having grasped the basic principles, are content to relegate them to the dimmer recesses of our minds. In any case, once you start sailing, understanding the theory soon takes second place to the actual implementation of it! The behaviour of a boat is governed by the wind, waves and the guiding hand of the helmsman, and the skill in that hand owes far more to sensitivity, observation and experience than to classroom tuition.

Whilst there is rarely any substitute for a skilled helmsman; so long as there is battery capacity available, electronic autopilots are invaluable for the mundane slog of passage making in settled weather and after the novelty of a full day at sea has worn off, there is conspicuously little fighting among the crew for a turn at the tiller! On longer passages, a mechanical wind vane gear can, under certain conditions, prove equal to all but the very best helmsman; generally the human hand is best when making to windward, while the self-steering proves superior on a dead run. This is because of the vane's reaction time: with the apparent wind from ahead, the helmsman senses it before the vane does, and vice versa when the wind is dead astern.

Airflow and pressure

Although stationary air exerts only the constant, atmospheric pressure, once it is in motion in the form of wind, it develops the kinetic energy that is used to drive a sailing vessel. As the wind flows over a sail, it becomes subject to variations in pressure: pressure being greatly reduced on the lee side and increased on the weather surface. It is this differential, directed by the sails, that produces a total force – the components being forward drive, heel and, unfortunately, drag as well.

It is not immediately obvious perhaps just how dramatic an

Light-weather sailing at its most enjoyable. Possibly a keen crew would have the boat heeled slightly to leeward to keep the sails full – and slightly reduce the hull's wetted surface. The headsail is set to a short plank bowsprit, the latest designer addition and de rigueur for sports boats, but in reality a pretty useless styling gimmick on any small boat, power or sail: it is vulnerable to damage and is good for little – except increasing harbour dues.

effect the variance between the negative and positive pressures can be, but when the atmospheric pressure of 2116 lb per sq ft (at sea level – which, presumably, is where the yacht in question actually is!) is lowered by, say, 3 lb per sq ft on the lee side, a sail area of 200 sq ft is subjected to 600 lb of suction – and this is the major component of the force acting upon the sails. Now, add to this a slightly weaker positive pressure of about 300 lb on the weather side and, since both forces are working in the same direction, that amounts to 900 lb of pressure acting on the sails – even though there is a gradient from luff to leech. In addition, there is a wind velocity gradient that must be taken into account: the speed of the airflow increases with height above the water, where the moving air is free from the slight friction of the sea surface.

It is easy enough to visualise the yacht being blown directly downwind, or even making good a course with the wind on the beam, but sailing to windward involves complex pressure interactions: the negative pressure is, as stated, the most critical and is caused by the airflow being first of all attracted and then, since it is incompressible, channelled and accelerated by the convex surface of the lee side of the sail – always with the pressure differential being most pronounced at the luff and tailing away towards the leech. Up to a point, that is. Should the curvature of the sail become too sharp, the deflected airstream will break away and join once more with the parallel flow of the unrestricted air. This creation of negative pressure becomes self-promulgating for, as more air reaches the leading edge of the sail, so it is in turn attracted by the zone of the decreased pressure and rushes to join up with it. The greater mass consequently fights to take up more space, so increasing the speed of the airflow even more; and so it goes on, creating an ever-increasing suction effect. All the time this is happening, of course, there is correspondingly less airflow on the weather side of the sail.

This is fine so far as it goes, but turning theory into actuality depends to a large degree upon the skill of the sailmaker – and of helmsman and sail trimmer. In other words, not only the cut of the sail, but also the angle of attack in relation to the wind, ensure the boat's efficiency under sail.

The taller the rig, the greater this efficiency since an appreciably greater proportion of the sail area will be in the less disturbed air higher up. A clean aerodynamic profile with minimal wind resistance also helps, with an elliptical profile being reckoned the best – though admittedly this is difficult to combine with practicality. (Perhaps the closest approach was in the pre-bent, curved 'hockey stick' masts seen in some of the early 30 square metre class and approximated by some flexible modern rigs.) Since, however, the average cruiser's rig is likely to be of low-aspect ratio and modest area, the cut and the camber or draft of the sails will be very important. This fullness gives the sail something of the aerodynamic qualities of an aircraft wing (or a bird's wing for that matter), and has a pronounced effect upon the flow of air, determining first of all whether that flow will be smooth or turbulent. The camber also determines the point at which the negative flow will break free: clearly, the further aft the maximum point of the camber is, the longer the airflow can be captured and the greater the drive produced for a given wind strength and point of sailing. It is less complicated than it sounds – but only slightly! Picture the yacht in stays, head-to-wind: the sails flog and no drive whatsoever is developed. Now, bear away slightly, haul in the sheets and the sails, take up a smooth aerodynamic curvature and start to draw; free off the sails too much, though, and the flow separates with random eddies developing – and the effect can be seen as the after edge of the sail and the leech begin to shake and lose power, or stall out.

Unfortunately, the sheer mechanics of the rig mean that it can never hope to attain aerodynamic perfection; the foresail comes nearest to this as it operates in air free from wind shadow. However, square foot for square foot, a long-luffed headsail produces between a third and 50 per cent more drive on the wind than does a Bermudan mainsail (a gaff main produces proportionally less – but add a jackyarder and things begin to even out). One reason for the relatively low drive of the mainsail is that it operates in the wind shadow of the mast with all the unavoidable turbulence – which explains why competitive craft go to such lengths to keep spar dimensions to the minimum. Yet it may also be backwinded by the headsail itself; indeed, very often – to a greater or lesser degree – this does happen. Backwinding is usually a pretty clear indication of badly cut sails or poorly sited sheet leads, but it can equally well be due to an inexperienced helmsman – or half-hearted hauling in of the sheets!

Since the foresail takes the leading role when working to windward, the cut must be as near perfect as it can be, and the sheeting angles optimal. The aim is to derive the utmost profit from the so-called 'slot effect', whereby the airflow is constricted by the curve of the headsail leech at the point of overlapping the mainsail luff. The physical laws governing the behaviour of air under pressure are coerced into preventing the mainsail luff from backwinding; this then leaves its own area of negative pressure free from turbulence – so further increasing the suction and helping to produce yet more forward drive.

To a large extent, the draft of the main should be related to the design of the working foresail: where this is short in the foot, without overlap (as a self-tacking jib would inevitably be), it cannot assist in smoothing the airflow to the mainsail; thus it helps if the latter is cut with the camber further aft than would otherwise be the case. However, the majority of masthead sloops set headsails with a good deal of overlap, and here the camber would be expected to be further forward. As sails age, they tend to bag somewhat, especially those of lighter cloth; and although Terylene sails rarely lose their shape completely, extra attention must be paid to adjustment. Old sails that have been re-cut to suit drastic alterations in rig (usually by the simple expedient of lopping off a chunk of foot and/or luff) may also have lost the flow, or have what remains of it after surgery too far aft for efficiency. Money invested in new sails, specifically cut to requirements, will prove to be money very well spent.

Controlling the draft

Draft can, of course, be altered to an extent by tensioning the luff, foot and leech: windward ability in particular being adversely affected by a slack luff to main or foresail. All but the very smallest of micro yachts would, in all likelihood, rely upon a halyard winch to tension the headsail luff and a combination of muscle power and a downhaul on the gooseneck for the main. In the absence of a halyard winch, a tack downhaul is worth fitting to the headsail, and quite often a tackle incorporating a jamming block – such as is commonly used for a kicking strap – is most convenient. Another option is a backstay tensioner for a small yacht; this would probably be in the form of a downhaul acting on a span or else pulling twin backstays together. An adjuster on the rigging screw of a single backstay also works well, but banish all thoughts of hydraulics – these come into the category of overkill!

It is fashionable to take all halyards aft to winches and rope clutches on the coachroof; if the halyards are internal, they are normally led via sheaves at the foot of the mast, with turning blocks if these are needed for a fair lead. External halyards are usually brought aft via deck blocks at the mast heel – and it is imperative that these are of the swivelling non-tumbling type or else they may jam, capsize – or both! On the whole, there is much to be said for leading everything to hand in the cockpit, but it is not always possible to achieve as tight a luff as might be desirable with a more direct purchase. This is especially true in the case of rope (rather than wire to rope) halyards.

The primary draft control of the headsail's leech and foot is the sheet, with the correct adjustment tension and angle of this being arguably the decisive factor in the boat's performance on the wind and in medium to heavy airs. In simplest terms, bringing the position of the sheet lead aft tightens the foot of the sail, thereby flattening the lower section and allowing

Twin headsails

Twin headsail rigs have long been popular running down the Trade Wind routes but are quite well suited to a downwind passage in a small cruiser. Though not unaffected by slight variations in wind, there is no danger from an accidental gybe and, without the weight of the mainsail and boom, there will be less rolling, too. For serious passage making, which in a small boat can be regarded as anything over thirty miles, it is worth taking the trouble to provide a means of reducing sail area when necessary; some well tried and tested types of reefing are sketched here.

If there is one point to bear in mind, it is that with twin staysails set, it will take time to put the boat about so a man overboard would be at considerable risk. It would also be ill-advised to run downwind with such a rig at night in shipping lanes – or in any congested waters at any time.

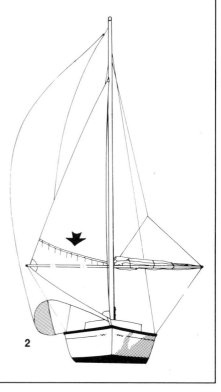

1 The Otway Waller system. Here, the running booms remain in position and the luff of the headsail is made fast to, and furled from, the outboard end of each. Drawbacks are that the booms must be of fairly substantial section and even when these are well stayed, there may still be too much twist and luff sag to operate the furling gear easily. Of the three types shown, this will also produce the worst rolling motion under reduced canvas.

2 The method used by Marin Marie in his singlehanded Atlantic crossing in *Winnibelle*. He replaced the boomless gaff mainsail by a spinnaker, set in conjunction with two moderate-sized running staysails and relied upon variations in sail area to self-steer the boat for long periods.

It worked well and had the advantage that, with reef points instead of roller furling, there was nothing to malfunction or jam. However, on a small yacht, the foredeck work might be demanding.

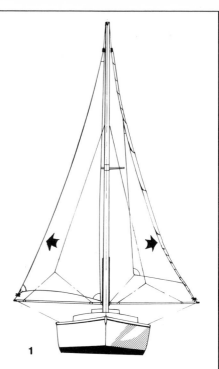

3 A good system for the smaller boat with the headsails in line, although there must be sufficient separation for the furling gear to operate freely. In this sketch, the jib is set on a bowsprit but for a small cruiser a detachable inner forestay would prove a better answer. With the smallest craft, it might be possible to dispense with lifts on the booms but, if they do sag once the sails are reefed, clearly it will be necessary to rig one. With sails furled or reefed sails on to the forestays and closer to the yacht's centreline, rolling will be less than either of the other two methods.

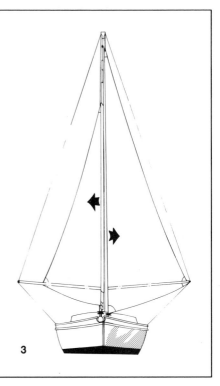

3

more curve in the leech. This in turn reduces the draft higher up the sail as well: move the sheet lead forward and the reverse is true. Though this tenet of sail trim is well known, it is not unusual for leads to be sited not only incorrectly, but also immovably with no provision for alteration either in the fore-and-aft plane or transversely. Equally common is for reefing headsails to be sheeted to tracks and leads capable of only minimal alteration – and this for an area that may vary between 50–150 sq ft (4.6–13.9 sq m)! And then there are, of course, leads cunningly sited so that the sail fouls the shrouds no matter what!

The first thing to get right is the lead from clew to fairlead in moderate winds; this always used to be easy to ascertain with mitre-cut sails because the sheet followed precisely the angle of the mitre and so exerted an even pressure. Where the sail is made with horizontal cloths, it may take some experimentation to make certain that there is no uneven pressure on leech or foot that could cause creases in the fabric, and so create the turbulence that will disrupt the all-important negative pressure to leeward. Yet once the fore-and-aft plane has been decided, and due provision made for different headsail sizes, it remains only to decide just how far inboard the leads should be placed, and here too trial and error will be the order of the day. Ideally, when hauled in, the sail should shiver only very slightly, but evenly, along the length, from head to foot. Since in strong winds the leads need to be further inboard than in light airs, sidedeck tracks that are aligned parallel with the yacht's centreline are clearly inferior to those with a degree of strategic curvature, for this makes it possible for the smaller foresail (partially reefed sail) set in gusty conditions to be sheeted well inboard while the larger sail used in light or moderate wind strengths can be led from a point aft and slightly closer to the gunwale. An alternative is to fit a pair of parallel tracks to each side with a transverse track and adjuster sliding fore-and-aft along them – though whether this actually would justify the complication and expense for a cruising boat is debatable. Barber haulers are one more possibility, and the most effective for the small cruising yacht.

Although it is normal practice to provide a leech tensioning line on large genoas and also on roller reefing headsails, such a refinement is not always considered necessary on the average working jib of a cruising boat. However, if there is one, a little judicious tension brought to bear can induce the airflow slightly aft: if you overtighten the leech, though, the flow will be upset with consequent turbulence backwinding the main. (If the headsail is cut with a leech hooking noticeably in on itself, this will have a deleterious effect on windward performance and may help induce a weather helm: the sail should be returned to the maker immediately.)

On the wind

When sailing hard on the wind, the main does contribute rather less drive than the foresail, but it is equally important to take some pains with the adjustment for a sail that sets poorly is a source of constant irritation to the helmsman and dispiriting for a keen crew – don't give up just because the sails are old and may have lost some of the original shape, even these will respond to a bit of tweaking!

As in the case of the headsail, the luff should be as taut as possible for windward work; however, if the mast is very flexible, maintaining the tension can require constant adjustment as a result of the stretch factor of rope: even racing dinghies with wire to rope halyards often fit a lock at the masthead to reduce this, but this is an invitation to trouble if the sail needs to be lowered in a hurry! Incidentally, if ordering new sails, do let the sailmaker know how much mast bend there is; with one-designs or production boats, precise measurements are

A Swift 18 on the wind in about 10 knots of breeze: nicely trimmed foresail, but the main is rather poorly set as evidenced by the girts in the sail from the clew to the first batten; the leech too is uneven with 'hard spots' around each batten.

generally readily available, but this will not be so with a one-off – or possibly an ex-racing boat. With a very bendy rig, it is best to have the sail precisely 'tailored' to the spars, otherwise deep diagonal creases – girts – may form in the cloth extending from the clew to a point about two-thirds of the height of the sail when the sheet is hauled in.

The Cunningham hole is one way of applying yet more tension to the luff: this is a simple but effective fitting, requiring only a cringle in the sail about 6 in (15.2 cm) above, and in line with, the tack eye. With it, a direct pull can be exerted by means of a downhaul to deck or boom. Although until fairly recently this would have been regarded as nothing more than a whimsical conceit borrowed from the dinghy racing fraternity, the difference it can make to sails set on the wind is now appreciated as crews grow more knowledgeable and rigs more responsive to even basic tuning.

Because flattening the sails brings the draft further forward and shifts the centre of effort aft, care must be taken to keep the camber where it is most beneficial – slightly forward of the middle part is about the optimum, for if it is induced too far forward, drive will be adversely affected. Things are slightly complicated by the natural tendency of the centre of effort to shift even further aft in stronger winds, and this has the effect of increasing weather helm and also, incidentally, the heeling moment. In order to achieve the best possible set, it is helpful to take up slightly on the clew outhaul (if this is possible – in practice, it may be hard to alter under load, so try to anticipate wind strength before setting out).

Naturally, each of the draft controls is interdependent to a degree, and it is in attempting to balance the amount of camber, its position and the twist in the sail that offers such a challenge to the crew. The twist of the sail, like the camber, can work with or against the crew, though the often heard and heated discussions on sail trim would seem to suggest that twist in a sail is to be ruthlessly eliminated at any cost! Excessive twist undoubtedly can cause the sail to lift and lose drive, and the temptation is always desperately to haul in the mainsheet even though this will do more harm than good, since it increases the angle of heel and exacerbates weather helm. However, a certain amount of twist is actually necessary higher up in the sail – roughly from a point level with the hounds upwards – thus allowing the best possible angle of attack relative to the airflow aloft, this air being less disturbed, but also a few degrees freer than at deck level.

As wide a mainsheet track as is compatible with the design of the yacht is one of the most effective aids to mainsail trim,

Light weather sailing

In light airs, achieving the best performance, or even any forward motion, calls for total concentration. Try to keep crew weight out of the ends of the boat and, in particular, never allow the transom to drag. If the rudder is one which lifts vertically, raising it slightly will reduce drag – but keep your eyes peeled for any approaching signs of breeze – quite strong gusts can come with little warning at the top of the tide on a hot summer's afternoon. Heeling the boat to leeward will, depending upon the design of the hull, usually reduce the wetted surface slightly and will at least encourage the sails to keep a full and stable curve. Don't, however, induce an angle of heel so sharp that rubbing strakes, chainplates or other clutter are immersed – and the rudder isn't! And watch out for weed on the rudder; if the wake or current running past the boat seems more turbulent than might be expected, weed could be the reason – not that it is always possible to do much about it, short of going for a swim armed with a broom!

Halyards are best set up fairly hard on the wind and freed very slightly off it, the mainsail should be eased away slightly, too. Don't be tempted to set up the kicking strap too tightly – in fact it may pay to take up a fraction on the topping lift to prevent the boom end from dragging. Try not to oversheet or fiddle with the sails, stillness is best; that said, keep alert for slight lifts or shifts in wind direction. Use lighter sheets on the foresail and replace clew shackles with the lightest links possible; a great lump of forged bronze or steel can be quite enough to prevent the sail drawing. If really keen, reduce the number of blocks in the mainsheet purchase to allow quicker response; a wire strop from boom to mainsheet is often used by the super-keen to reduce the length, and therefore the weight, of the mainsheet.

Some small cruisers develop pronounced lee helm in very light airs and cannot be persuaded to hold any course at all. If this proves to be the case, it may be worth changing down to a smaller headsail; otherwise, simply make the best of it and anchor. Eventually the breeze will fill in, though be prepared for a change of direction.

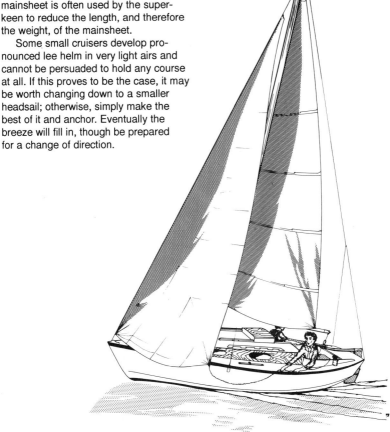

since the angle of attack can be adjusted without any need to free off, or, just as bad, to oversheet the sail. Yet to be of any real assistance this track really must be a minimum of 3 ft (91 cm) in width. Obviously, it works better if the mainsheet attachment is midway along the boom rather than at the outhaul, but with some masthead rigs, where there is only a small mainsail area, this is not practicable. (With such a short boom, there is a strong possibility that its outer end will be about in line with the helm position and also at just about face height – as can be imagined, there is great potential to inflict a serious injury.)

Although full-width tracks would normally only be seen on dedicated racing craft, abbreviated versions – something of a fashion accessory on many cruisers – don't really fulfil any purpose; one only has to look at coamings or accommodation bulkheads to see how often there are signs of chafe, grooves worn, even in GRP, by the mainsheet at the extent of the travel! However, assuming the track is wide and unencumbered enough to use, ensure that the traveller slides freely and that its position can be altered under load (a unit with captive ball races is far superior); and also that it has control lines and purchases rather than spring-loaded adjustable stops, since the action of these is inclined to seize after prolonged exposure to salt spray.

If a centreline mainsheet track is used in conjunction with a mainsheet attachment to the boom's midpoint, it takes over some of the function of the kicking strap; indeed, on a cruiser it could really be considered as a viable alternative. If converting from an aft mainsheet to a central system, remember that the loading upon the boom and fittings is considerable and make absolutely certain that the spar is up to it.

The kicking strap for offwind sailing

The kicking strap (often mistakenly referred to as a boom vang, for the latter is really a preventer led forward from the boom to minimise the chaos that can be wrought by an unintended gybe) has evolved from the most basic handy-billy to mega-tackle, strut or hydraulic systems, some of which are powerful enough to pull half the coachroof out by the roots – and this has been known to happen, although it is more usual for the boom to snap in half first!

This particular item of the rig is designed to stop the boom lifting when sailing off the wind, and it really earns its keep on a dead run in moderate to heavy airs. As it counteracts the tendency of the boom to point skywards, it also prevents excessive twist in the upper part of the main; and twist, with the wind dead aft, causes some of the sail to blow forward of the mast and so, in effect, to leeward – a situation that can result in a spectacular Chinese gybe or the build-up of a horrendous weather roll. True, in magazine photos racing crews can be seen scrambling up the deck with grins of glee as the boom aims at the heavens and the spinnaker turns into a glorified sea anchor, but they are of course enjoying themselves at the owner's expense (and owners of ocean racers are not exactly notorious for poverty!). A weather roll must be stopped before the motion has time to accelerate out of control, and before real damage to the gear is sustained: this is achieved easily enough by hauling in the mainsheet and luffing slightly. Take care, though, not to bear away even further by mistake; if the helmsman is sitting to leeward rather than his or her more customary position to weather, this is very easy to do and will in a strong wind almost inevitably bring about a broach.

Common sense rather than cowardice would suggest that the skipper of a small cruising yacht would hardly be tempted to carry so much sail, and in such a wind force, as to let this state of affairs develop, but there is always the chance that the breeze may rise gradually and without the crew immediately being aware of it. When passage making offshore, the increase in size of the waves would probably be warning enough, and in any case, if there is no other boat in the vicinity, there is less inclination to show off (something most of us are prone to do on occasion!).

Offwind sailing is generally thought to call for less skill and concentration than upwind work, and helmsmen often tend to excel at one at the expense of the other. Certainly a minor error of judgement is pretty apparent when making to windward (though the same could be said when running by the lee!), but reaching and running both require good judgement and an intuitive approach; it is easy to get a yacht to perform acceptably on a reach, but fine adjustment of the sails is needed to achieve that final edge. On a dead run, the major concern is to get all sails drawing in clear air, without blanketing each other. When making a passage in a fresh breeze, the majority of small yachts would be as well (or sometimes better off) without the mainsail, since the weight of the boom increases the tendency to roll – and in many masthead-rigged craft, the mainsail is too small to contribute much in the way of drive. Whenever possible, the headsail should be boomed out – whether or not it is set in conjunction with the main. If the wind is fluky and the sail reluctant to stay out to weather, collapsing as the boat rolls, it is often worth booming it out on the leeward side where it may settle to work quite happily; this is not permitted under racing rules, though goodness knows why not! When sailing in unobstructed waters, the best arrangement for a cruiser is twin staysails; even in very fresh conditions, so long as these are cut fairly high in the foot, they will give a smoother and better balanced ride. Don't forget, though, that with these set and boomed out, manoeuvrability will be restricted and a sharp alteration in course cannot be carried out on the instant. These sails are very powerful and should be handled with the care that would be accorded a spinnaker or cruising chute; the booms, although usually on the light side, should nevertheless (in all but the very smallest boats) be fitted with lift and downhaul.

Sailing with a spinnaker

In spite of the awe in which spinnakers seem to be held, on a dead run in wind strengths of up to about 15 knots, they are easy to set, trim and dowse and can actually make the yacht more tractable; after all, the faster the boat travels with the wind astern, the lower the apparent wind filling the sail.

There are several ways of controlling spinnakers during the critical stages of hoisting and lowering (ie those stages most conducive to anxiety attacks in less practised crews), although most of the mental and physical stress can be avoided by undertaking both operations with the spinnaker safely in the wind shadow of the mainsail.

The spinnaker of a small cruiser is unlikely to be much over 300 sq ft (27.8 sq m) in area, set on a boom that has (or should have) identical piston fittings at each end. The boom, always set on the opposite side to the mainsail, clips on to a ring sliding within a short track on the fore part of the mast, and is controlled, on a small yacht, by a lift and downhaul – while a guy and sheet trim the sail itself; if the spinnaker is to be set very 'shy' – with the wind only just aft of the beam – a jockey pole or strut may also be needed to relieve the strain on the pole and to keep the guy from fouling the shrouds. Simple, isn't it? In practice, although the spinnaker is double clewed and set flying, it pays to think of it as no more than a large headsail, with a leech and luff like any other.

There are several ways of setting the sail, a number with the assistance of ingenious accessories or gadgetry: these range from a zippered bag that is actually part of the sail, by a snuffer or squeezer (which contains the sail until the moment of truth), or 'high-tec' (as with Gary Hoyt's 'gun-mount' system, where the boom slides within a pivoting sleeve fixed to the pulpit). Yet simplest of all is to hoist straight out of a reinforced bag known as a 'turtle' – substitutes for which include plastic dustbins and linen baskets! Whatever the chosen container, it is then clipped to foredeck, stanchions or main hatch; the sail can also be launched through a chute or directly through the forehatch in light weather. If using a turtle (or setting directly from deck or hatch), the sail should be put in stops first; this entails carefully dividing the material into three rolled sections, one from each clew and one from the head to about the mid-point (so the sail takes on the appearance of a three-pointed star). Each of these sections is then tied with either elastic bands or lightweight thread (traditionally 'rotten cotton' was employed bought specially for the purpose from all chandlers) and, as the sail is hoisted, the wind will snap these out and the sail will fill, little by little. That's the theory, and in practice, so long as the material has been portioned accurately (and the stops are not too strong), and also that both sheet and guy have been checked in case they have got tangled with lifelines, shrouds or each other, this method has a high success rate with only a minimal chance of the spinnaker developing that famous hour-glass twist that so fascinates spectators! If setting the sail on a reach from stops, it may be best to do so from the main hatch, with one member of the crew feeding the length out gradually.

When it comes to lowering the sail, the object (needless to say) is to keep it from dropping over the side! Accepted practice is to ease away the luff, while at the same time hauling in the leeward clew, so bringing the sail in tightly – and in the shelter of the mainsail. Next, release the pole and haul in the leech leaving the luff flying; then haul the sail inboard, keeping tension on the leech (which has now, in effect, changed places with the luff). If necessary, alter course slightly so as to keep the sail blanketed during lowering; the sail then has even less chance of escaping and one person should be able to manage the drop within a few moments. (Whereupon a crew member should immediately be detailed to confine it once more to stops, ready for hoisting!)

Quite a few racing keel boats and dinghies control the spinnaker set and drop by using an underdeck chute and restraining line: the sail is held partly in check during both operations by this line, which is attached to a reinforced patch on the spinnaker, a little over half-way up; when hoisting, this tends to prevent the sail flying wild, and while tweaking, it pulls the lowered spinnaker neatly back into the chute. The idea could well be adapted to suit the small cruiser, although clearly a

The 'gun-mount' spinnaker system devised by Gary Hoyt. Simple in concept – the spinnaker boom simply slides through a swivelling collar mounted on the deck or pulpit – it does tame the spinnaker effectively, although restricting the pole length.

watertight unit might be expensive to construct.

The purist might argue that snuffers or squeezers have taken all the fun out of handling spinnakers – and cruising chutes too – for the sail is sent aloft confined in the nylon tube in which it is stowed, the tube having a wide mouth or ring at the lower end; once the sail is up (but still encased), the mouth is hoisted until it clears the head of the sail, the sail so being released. To lower, the ring is downhauled and simply swallows up the sail, stowing it once more within the sock. Apart from the fact that the snuffer remains clearly visible at the masthead, the system is as near perfect as it could be; if there is a drawback, it is the cost – which is quite a high proportion of the actual sail price.

Asymmetric spinnakers, immensely powerful on a reach, are another import from the dinghy and skiff racing scene, but they adapt well to the needs of the micro yacht by virtue of the relative simplicity: the boom, when not in use, retracts into the hull; when the spinnaker is set, the boom is duly extruded, doing away with lifts and downhauls and leaving the crew to concentrate on the sail trim.

Spinnakers vary in cut, with the best for general duty being the radial head or tri-radial types – though the latter is considerably more expensive. Both are stable when set and can be carried quite close to the wind. Once a spinnaker is correctly trimmed and the pole height adjusted – except in variable or gusty winds – there should not be much call to fiddle incessantly with the sheet and guy; this often causes the sail to collapse on itself anyway. It would be asking for trouble, though, to disappear below and leave everything to its own devices: not only is there a chance that, with an unexpected wind shift, the spinnaker might take charge of the boat, but the crew in the cockpit must keep their eyes peeled too: the sail impedes vision and obscures from view such menaces as hydrofoils and high-speed ferries (not to mention other yachts) that may be relentlessly following their preordained courses. All in all, though, a well-set spinnaker is surprisingly tolerant, and will even run by the lee for some time before gybing can no longer be put off.

Gybing the spinnaker

'Put off' it frequently is, even though there is nothing inherently difficult about the operation – at least, not after the first couple of attempts, which should take place in light winds. However, it is one occasion where sure-footedness on the foredeck is needed – most small yachts, being sensitive to weight on the foredeck, will either luff sharply or simply put the snout under the nearest handy wave. Though only a minority of cruisers would carry a spinnaker in boisterous conditions, a rising wind can nevertheless catch everyone unawares. Gybing in winds of much above 15 knots calls for confidence, but the procedure varies little and familiarity with it breeds confidence rather than contempt: using the normal end-for-end procedure (assuming that there are identical fittings at both ends of the pole), the first move is to unclip the pole from the mast – having first ensured that the lift is set up. Next, clip the pole on to the sheet (which will now become the new guy) before freeing it from the old guy. At this point, the pole is attached to both control lines, but not the mast, so just unclip the old guy, push out the sail to weather, and snap the pole back on to the mast, then haul in and trim – nothing to it! Seriously, though gybing is simple enough, a lot depends on having a helmsman who can be relied upon to keep on course, and also, in the absence of a third pair of hands, to trim the sail so that it continues to draw throughout the operation; once it collapses about the ears of the foredeck crew, it can take a bit of disentangling.

When sailing with the wind dead aft, as though a spinnaker

were not enough to keep the crew happily occupied, there are various 'gap-fillers' that can be hung up as well; these range from a double-clewed 'banana staysail', a 'tall boy' (which is narrower and somewhat flatter), through to a common or garden working jib. For that little extra challenge, the spinnaker can be balanced (or if the crew loses concentration, momentarily, unbalanced) by a 'blooper', which is a very light, full-cut genoa, essentially not dissimilar to some cruising chutes. In fact, I have used one sail for both purposes, which would no doubt raise eyebrows among sailmakers! It is argued that such sails have no place on a cruising boat, and possibly it might not be worthwhile to make a point of purchasing them from new. However, over the years, many yachts accumulate a comprehensive, if rather eclectic, sail wardrobe as successive owners buy and discard sails at whim: so, why not set them? To this end, after all, these working craft sported jackyarders, jib topsails, primitive spinnakers, squaresails – occasionally with raffees above these – watersails and ringtails; a sailing vessel is intended to derive the maximum benefit from all that air in motion!

Nowadays, it is the ubiquitous cruising chute, spinoa or gennikker (the same concept is behind all of these very full lightweight headsails) that has in most cases superseded the cruiser's normal light-weather complement of ghoster, genoa and spinnaker. True, this sail, a very full lightweight genoa, set flying rather than being hanked on to the forestay, can be easier to set than a spinnaker. It is at its best on a reach up to about Force 3 – at which point the crew of a small cruiser would probably start thinking about changing down to the working jib. On a run, the sail, in common with a spinnaker, would need to be set on a pole, and since generally a cruising chute is comparable in size, this pole would of necessity be strong and also complete with lift and downhaul – hence the cost and complexity approach those of a spinnaker. On a reach, though, there is no doubt that it is rather easier to set and retrieve, but it should be borne in mind at all times that a cruising chute is nevertheless a large and relatively fragile sail – and as such, it has to be treated with respect.

When sailing in light weather, such sails can call for almost as much delicacy of touch, for given a brief lapse in wind strength, they are prone to collapse – and not many things are as dispiriting as trying to encourage several hundred square feet of drooping, flamboyantly coloured rip-stop nylon into some semblance of life! In the faintest of airs, a ghoster is probably at least as efficient and, on a reach, heeling the boat to leeward (or what would be leeward if there were any wind) will cause both main and headsail to adopt a fuller curve, and so make the most of any passing air currents. The handling of the boat counts too, and unless racing, there is only one option when the wind dies away: move the crew forward to ensure that the transom is clear of the water (and not therefore creating unnecessary drag), to issue dire warnings against all unnecessary changes in sail trim or over-zealous movements of the rudder, and also to prohibit conversation lest it disturb the concentrated scanning of clouds and water for signs of a breeze.

Getting caught up in an adverse tidal stream with no engine does instil a feeling of helplessness; within the confines of a river, if a long sweep is carried, it should be feasible to scull across the current – and with luck, close inshore there may be a helpful counter stream, or at any rate the flow will be less strong. Keeping a pair of oars or sweeps aboard is always a wise precaution, even when there is an auxiliary engine. It should be quite possible to paddle or even to row – either singlehanded or double-handed depending upon the length of the oars and the beam of the yacht. In coastal waters, anchoring may be an option, but otherwise (apart from establishing the rate of drift and checking your position regularly) there is little to do: calms catch out as many yachts as gales, and provision should be made for them!

Some of the more esoteric light-weather sails will need winches for sail trimming; those for a cruising chute or spinnaker are really best mounted well aft unless there is room for a turning block on deck – in which case it will be possible to lead sheet or guy to existing headsail winches. However, if fitting out a glassfibre boat from scratch or refitting an older craft, it is as well to make future provision for these extra items of hardware by glassing-in reinforcing pads – sooner or later, after a few peaceful hours spent waiting for a fresh breeze, an awful lot of people do succumb to the lure of spinnakers and cruising chutes, for these at least give skipper and crew the illusion that they are in control of their destiny when the wind dies!

6 Storm Sails and Heavy Weather

The tri-sail

Storm sails are of course rather less enticing, for they remind the crew of any vessel (but especially the crew of a small yacht) that they and their craft are at the mercy of the weather. It could be that storm jib, and sometimes tri-sail too, are really bought as an insurance policy – 'if we have them, that guarantees we'll never need them!' – and this is why they are often so indifferently cared for. Yet no matter how immaculate the other sails are, it is a constant source of surprise to see well-made and expensive storm sails hauled out during a survey: cringles corroded right away, the fabric stained with damp and rust from the luff wire (or galvanised strop and shackle), and piston hanks so heavily encrusted with salt as to be immovable except with penetrating oil and pliers! Tri-sails with slides that don't fit track or groove – and for which there is no provision on mast or deck – are equally common. Clearly, such sails are in no condition to be set in a hurry – if at all.

It is always advisable to reduce sail before the weather really deteriorates, before the onset of darkness, and before the crew grow too tired to care about it one way or the other. Yet prior to this, those on board should have checked the sails and ensured that there are sheets made fast to the storm jib (definitely *not* with a snap shackle) and also a tack strop for the sail (this is important as it should be set higher than either the working headsail or genoa in order to keep clear from waves or heavy spray). Check that the piston hanks are free, also necessary shackles, and make certain that the fairleads are correctly adjusted.

Accepted practice when setting a tri-sail (which tends to be thought of, quite erroneously, as a sail to be set only in desperation) is initially to make the mainboom fast on to a gallows or, leaving it still attached to the gooseneck, to lash the outer end securely on deck. The tri-sail is, as the name implies, a very flat, heavy sail of triangular cut, although a few gaff-

Charles Stock's well-known 16 ft (4.8 m) gaff cutter Shoal Waters, *with a storm tri-sail set in a full gale. Although most gaff-rigged vessels would opt for a jib-headed tri-sail, that of Shoal Waters is set to a short gaff. Note the sail is sheeted on to the quarter with its own sheet. The jib is noticeably flat in cut, although surprisingly the tri-sail has quite a bit of flow. Sensibly, there is a brailing line to the mast that can depower the sail immediately if necessary.*

rigged yachts do favour a sail with a small gaff rather than the usual jib-headed version. Occasionally, for ease in hoisting, the sail is set with parrel lines secured by toggles and provided with balls to prevent friction, but it is more usual nowadays for it to be set on to the main track (or luff groove) where it either bypasses the gooseneck by a supplementary track, or may be set on a short separate length of track (though this would be unusual in a small yacht). In fact, in a small craft, the boom is far better removed from the gooseneck altogether and lashed along the sidedeck, because its excess windage is highly undesirable and would certainly exacerbate leeway and heeling. The sail is sheeted to the quarters – and sheeted in hard; and while a tri-sail is most often set when lying hove-to, just so long as the sail can be carried safely and a slight measure of flow be maintained, it should be possible to make some progress to windward – or at least to hold on to any ground gained before the onset of a gale.

There is no hard-and-fast rule as to the point at which it becomes impossible (dangerous even) to keep any sail set; a small yacht obviously will not be able to thrash on for as long, and in such wind or wave forces, as a larger, heavier one. Eventually there will come a point at which forward motion is stopped dead by the angle of heel, the boat perhaps even repeatedly knocked down, and the alternatives then are to lie hove-to if there is sea room to leeward or to run downwind (either under storm jib, bare poles or, if still travelling too fast, with warps towed astern). If these options are ruled out, the yacht may be forced to lie a'hull with no sail set.

Approaching gale: strategy planning

If the gale has been anticipated and the boat has been able to gain sufficient offing, there will be time to consider the best course of action; with a rocky coastline a mile or so down to leeward, it is all-important to keep the boat on the wind for as long as is humanly possible. So long as the angle of heel is not too great, then use the inboard if there is one; if there is an outboard, a steep head sea may render it ineffectual as the prop will constantly be thrown clear of the water. In either case, it has to be considered whether the engine might be better used only as a last resort; if it is inevitable that the yacht will be driven down on to a lee shore, in spite of all attempts to claw off, a few minutes under power might just make it possible to steer clear of such dangers as outcrops of rock, or even manmade obstructions.

First, the fuel reserve must be assessed with due allowance made for the fact that the engine, running hard (even racing at times), will develop an excessive thirst. It will be difficult to top up the tanks without chancing some water contamination, but if it can be done without risk, then do so. The reliability of the machinery must also be considered and overheating is a real possibility. If the yacht is at a steep angle of heel or the pitching severe, the raw water inlet will of course be irregularly submerged, so in consequence the flow of coolant will be interrupted. (Bear in mind, too, that a micro cruiser will certainly be more affected by the sea state than a larger vessel.) Also, there is a reasonable chance that the violence of the motion will stir up sediment in the tanks; diesel engines in particular are very intolerant of dirt or air in the system or a cessation of the fuel supply, however short-lived. (Even if no attempt has been made to refill tanks, don't discount the possibility, slim though it might seem, that a trickle of water may have found its way through the deck filler cap. Few such caps can be guaranteed to remain watertight if subjected to a deluge, or actually immersed, which in a gale is pretty well unavoidable from time to time.) If it comes to it, neither an outboard on the transom (or installed in a well), nor an inboard petrol engine, will take kindly to being swamped – an eventuality that cannot be discounted if attempting to make progress in heavy weather.

The decision as to when – or whether – to use the engine may be forced upon the boat, but if there is a breathing space before the final commitment, the skipper should think about the likelihood of rescue – whether from the shore or nearby shipping. If you are sure that your Mayday has been received or your distress flares sighted, do everything possible to keep to the sea since every moment will bring help nearer to hand, by lifeboat or helicopter. Faced with a deserted sea and desolate shoreline, immediate hopes of rescue might be slender, but still the best chance of ultimate safety is to keep the yacht at sea for as long as you can and by any means possible. Breaking waves, when observed from seaward, appear far smoother and flatter than they will be in reality, and though a sandy or shingled shore may not look particularly hazardous (in fact, it may even look enticing to a weary crew), any idea of safety is illusory. No yacht will withstand battering by onshore waves and, once grounded, it may offer only brief protection to the crew before breaking up.

Yet even when the situation seems hopeless, never give up: the ground tackle may still prevent the yacht going ashore, as history has shown so many times. With the anchor (or preferably anchors) on a long scope, there is a strong possibility that one will hold or snag around an underwater obstruction. At the very least, once the water shoals, an anchor drudging along the bed will slow progress, and every moment may bring help nearer.

This is the 'worst case scenario' – without which no book is complete! Sadly, tragedies do occur, but they are rare. Many of the minor upsets involving the rescue services could be avoided by using more common sense, and less 'radio-assisted panic': as yachts increasingly carry VHF, so there is growing reliance on the availability of the helping hand! (And, dare it be said, some rescuers, notably the inshore units, are a bit inclined to overreact at the slightest intimation of trouble, real or imaginary.)

All in all, though, few would deny that there are those

moments in everyone's sailing life where thoughts of survival
(or, if you prefer, intimations of mortality) are very much to the
fore, although after the event, the realisation usually dawns
that the worry was largely unjustified. It is perfectly possible to
cruise for half a lifetime and never be faced with more than
the occasional brisk summer gale – but luck does seem to play
a part, for equally there are those who appear to draw down
storms upon themselves (and those they sail with!).

With sea room to spare

Assuming that there is sea room and to spare, a gale should
not pose a more serious threat to the small cruiser than to a
larger vessel; it will be mainly a matter of sitting it out once the
yacht and crew have anticipated and prepared for everything
– including the unexpected. Gales can and do spring up with
little or no warning, but most build gradually in intensity, often
without the crew being aware of the actual wind velocity until
the yacht starts to stagger. To be on the safe side when passage making, no sooner is the first reef tucked in than it is time
to think about making everything secure down below and on
deck. If breakable objects can be hurled around, they will be:
drawers should be held closed with shock-cord; crockery and
pans not immediately needed should be wadded with cloths
to stop them crashing around; and all domestic gear surplus to
need stashed into lockers. Don't get carried away, though, and
hide any spares, tools or items of gear that might be needed in
a hurry. Wherever feasible, carry in the cabin duplicates of
small but vital items of deck and cockpit equipment: if there is
a knock-down and the winch or bilge pump handle, pliers,
torch (and flares) go overboard, though the loss of such trivia
might initially seem to be one of the least of the worries, it
could prove very serious later on.

Make certain that the bilges are pumped dry; it might be
thought that a few inches of water sloshing around will be
harmless enough, but not only is it unsettling, but it becomes
that much more difficult to check that there are no leaks
developing.

After checking the accommodation and, as far as possible,
the equipment on deck – security of stanchions, lifelines and
jackstays, as well as all rigging screws, sheet leads etc – take
time to prepare for the needs of the crew with flasks of hot soup
and sweet drinks. Just for once, ignore the advice of dietitian
and dentist: have to hand a supply of 'comfort food' such as
chocolate bars, fruit cake, perhaps dried fruit, for a sip of this

and a nibble of that at prescribed intervals helps pass the time. After using the cooker, ensure that the gas supply is turned off, and also that the cylinder cannot shift no matter what (if it is properly installed, of course, this should be impossible in any case!).

Delicate though the subject is, it is wise to think beforehand about what could – literally – be called rude health. Modesty is often so deeply instilled as to make bodily needs highly embarrassing, and since it is awkward to use the small lavatory of a micro yacht when heavily oilskinned, it is well to discuss matters openly even if the crew is normally more inhibited. On no account should anyone attempt to 'hang on', perhaps for hours on end: the discomfort impairs concentration and may lead to a painful urinary tract infection – a by no means uncommon, though little publicised, aftermath to a protracted gale.

Unless conditions deteriorate to the point where setting any sail whatsoever is out of the question, the yacht and crew will be most comfortable hove-to under backed storm jib and deep-reefed main or tri-sail. The term 'comfortable' is, admittedly, relative, but once the vessel is settled down – and a light fin-keel micro yacht may need more attention than a long-keeled vessel with deep forefoot – the motion will ease noticeably; and apart from occasional flogging of sails as the boat establishes a pattern of coming up to the wind then falling away, it will be fairly peaceful below.

The acquisition of at least some advance practice in setting the storm canvas will certainly be an asset if and when the time comes to do so in 'real life'! And the same goes for the technique of heaving-to in a reasonable weight of wind – don't forget that the boat's behaviour hove-to in waves and with storm jib and tri-sail may be less equable than when lying in settled weather with backed working jib and eased main while under way – as is habitual if, for example, the crew take five to prepare a snack under way.

Heaving-to

There is no question that some yachts are disinclined by design to lie hove-to at all, and light-displacement yachts – notably those with relatively high freeboard and shallow-sectioned hulls – are the worst offenders, almost always needing a hand on the tiller (though, in coastal waters, a watch would be kept in any case).

A yacht hove-to is not, of course, stationary in the water;

some headway will still be made, though the jib (set aback) reduces this to a minimum. Yet leeway will be quite pronounced, depending upon hull configuration along with the windage of topsides and rig – and such incidentals as the dodgers, spray cover, lifebelts, radar reflector, etc. Since leeway or drift may be as much as 2 or 3 knots (to be on the safe side, base calculations on the higher figure), the importance of adequate room to sit out the gale cannot be emphasised too strongly – this is, after all, the reason for squeezing every mile up to windward while able to do so.

If there is a choice – and unless well off soundings, there probably won't be – heave-to on the starboard tack: this theoretically gives you the right of way even if there is not much chance of needing to assert this!

Under storm sails, the balance of the rig should approximate that of the working sails – with the centre of effort in a similar position. Although a slight bias aft is not likely to have much effect on the yacht's behaviour, moving the centre of effort too far forward might be a very different matter, for in this case the boat may well pay off before the wind, accelerating and bringing the seas beam-on. Forward progress will be increased too; this is obviously undesirable since one reason for heaving-to is to avoid being deflected from the projected course. If the eventual destination of the cruise lies at safe distance downwind, the yacht would probably be running slowly towards it rather than lying hove-to. The yacht's angle relative to the breaking seas could heighten the possibility of a knockdown, or even of a 360 degree roll, and (at best) the unwanted speed increase due to the forereaching will cause the craft to pitch violently and bury the bows. Given a short and very steep wave system, the rudder of a small cruiser might be ineffective for much of the time, which would greatly add to the difficulty of maintaining any sort of control.

The main or tri-sail should be sheeted tightly home, with any residual drive (and there is bound to be some no matter how flat the sail is cut) being counteracted by the storm jib sheeted hard to weather. With a small yacht, it will be doubtful whether the helm can be left unattended, though in a perfect world it would be possible to leave the helm lashed down. When the yacht is hove-to, it forges slowly ahead, gradually edging up into the wind under the influence of the main: as soon as it comes up to the point when the sails start to luff, the backed headsail takes over and pushes the bows off the wind until the main once again begins to fill; this restful cycle is then repeated until conditions ease – or until the wind increases and it becomes necessary to consider other options.

Hove-to

Heaving-to in a small yacht is less comfortable than some articles written about heavy weather sailing might lead one to expect, but it should be an improvement on attempting vainly to struggle to windward. Only rarely, however, can the small yacht be left without a steadying hand on the tiller and, in coastal waters, it goes without saying that a lookout must be maintained at all times. It is essential that the watchkeeper be warmly dressed and, in the exposed cockpit of a small yacht, a dry suit should be worn. Otherwise, so-called 'deciduous' layered clothing will be best. Cockpit cushions are not merely a soft option, because they add warmth as well as comfort, but they must be adequately secured. Flasks of hot drinks filled before they are needed are essential – a half-cup of soup at regular intervals does much to keep spirits up. Boredom, nervousness and cold together quickly bring on exhaustion.

No yacht, large or small, should contemplate offshore – or even coastal – sailing without being prepared to spend a period hove-to. Where there is a furling headsail, a storm jib set from an inner stay should also be carried together with a storm tri-sail. With small craft, it is best to stow the main boom on deck or on the coachroof but it must be securely lashed as it is bound to be used as a handhold if the crew has to go forward. Under the rig shown in the sketch, the boat will continue to make some headway and this must be allowed for. When planning strategy be aware that gales vary in duration with the wind changing direction as well as strength.

Inset: Setting a spitfire jib aft, hanked on to a backstay, could help to keep the boat's head into the wind slightly and so improve the attitude when lying hove-to.

During the time spent in this way, apart from routine checks on hatches, bilges, rigging etc, a keen watch must be kept: weather that will force a small yacht to ease down or heave-to will hardly be noticed by, or act as a deterrent to, 60 000 tons of bulk carrier. Other yachts, large vessels in particular, can also be a danger; although not immune to gale force winds, they are of course less affected by them – and a gale that is seriously inconveniencing a small cruiser will quite likely be delighting the crew of a Whitbread racer! Sailing vessels pose an insiduous hazard: in favourable winds, they storm along at surprisingly high speeds, and though you might have some auditory warning of a three-masted barque coming up astern, an 80 ft (24.3 m) sloop runs almost silent. Furthermore, although such craft usually have powerful navigation lights, the height of these can be misleading, and what is in fact a yacht closing fast can easily be mistaken for a commercial vessel some distance off. (Bear in mind that a large ultra-light-displacement racer (or multihull) will clock up 20 knots plus at times – and that at such a time the crew may be more concerned with maintaining such a speed than looking out for small yachts (which, so the crew of the larger vessel might claim, have no business being in the area in the first place!) I was very nearly run down in a gale off the French coast by a yacht rattling along under spinnaker – the crew presumably being too preoccupied in keeping the sail from taking over to notice navigation lights under their bow.

A small yacht is vulnerable on two counts: on seeing and on being seen. By virtue of its relatively low freeboard, the crew's height of eye will be low at all times and the lively movement will give the lookout only spasmodic glimpses of the surrounding area as the boat crests waves; this greatly increases the difficulty in picking out, identifying or predicting the activities of any shipping that may be in the vicinity. At night, the problem is intensified. By the same token, the small vessel may be completely hidden from view in the trough of a wave and, to make matters worse, will produce only a faint radar echo (which may well be obscured by wave clutter anyhow). A reflector is vital, but even this will probably be only 15 ft (4.5 m) or so above the deck level and echoes may be intermittent depending upon the sea state – don't rely upon it being picked out on the screen.

Without doubt, the masthead tri-colour lights now fitted on yachts are a vast improvement over those diminutive items that used to decorate coachroof sides or the fore ends of pulpits; these were in any case mounted so low down as to be invisible from the bridge of a large vessel. Yet in heavy weather, the lights of a small boat may be difficult to distinguish, a fact made worse by the fading, discoloration or dirtiness of the lenses. Powerful lights consume amps at such an alarming rate as to encourage some skippers to switch on only in time of need, and there must have been numerous collisions as a result of inaccurate estimates as to the precise moment of necessity. That this practice is quite common, although not recommended (indeed illegal), was revealed years ago off the south Devon coast when I disobeyed orders to spare the batteries and illuminated the yacht. In response, the sea around was lit up, bright as a fairground. Yet it was for an instant only, then there was darkness once more: presumably, we had sailed straight through a foreign fleet fishing illicitly!

If you are seriously preoccupied by the presence of shipping, and doubtful whether the yacht can be seen, putting on spreader lights or a deck flood will settle the matter; this is not generally advised, though the main objection is the current consumption. Most important, the yacht will be seen and no vessel is going to steer deliberately on a collision course with an unidentified white light (though it may sidle over for a closer look). To my mind, spreader lights and/or a powerful searchlight that can be directed on the sails are essential safety equipment for any small boat sailing offshore. (It is often suggested that storm sails are best made in high visibility orange, but this will not show up so well at night, even with light directed upon them. Yet there is a good case for sewing reflective patches on to storm sails – or, for that matter, all working cruising sails.)

Recommended practice on the approach of anything large and sinister is to shine a torch into wheelhouse or bridge or, in extremis, to send up a white flare. However, don't leave it until the last moment; the helmsman of the other ship, perhaps startled from a pleasant reverie and in panic, may alter course towards the yacht rather than away. I have known this happen, and came close to losing the yacht off Finisterre, an area notable for the flow of commercial ships with lackadaisical watchkeepers (or, so rumour has it, none at all).

In strengthening winds

If the wind continues to strengthen, the yacht will in theory have two choices. The first is to run downwind with all sails taken off, under bare poles; if the speed is too high, and as a consequence the boat is constantly on the point of broaching (or pitchpoling, which in a fine-bowed boat with a buoyant stern cannot be discounted), the recommended procedure is then to slow progress by trailing warps (or a sea anchor) astern. Unfortunately, like so much advice, though this is held to work for every yacht in theory, the actuality could be very different – and there is no way of knowing that beforehand. A light-displacement fin-keeled yacht is not, at the best of times, the most directionally stable hull configuration and could well yaw wildly under the influence of the warps, even when these are streamed in a bight, made fast to both quarters. In a small yacht, sensitive to weight aft, there is always the added danger of the rope pinning the stern down, perhaps even directly causing the vessel to be pooped – with a wave raking the hull from stern to bow. The weight and drag of even those relatively light warps that would be carried as an essential part of the small cruising yacht's normal inventory is quite remarkable, and will of course impose both snatch and direct strains on the quarter cleats – stresses that the nylon or plastic type frequently supplied as standard on numerous small production craft are unlikely to withstand (even if the cleats do, the fastenings and backing pads may not!). However, even under bare poles, the windage of hull and rig may keep the boat moving too fast for safety, and warps provide a fairly effective and controllable braking system. But if there is a risk of driving down on to a lee shore, more drastic measures would have to be taken and it might be necessary to try towing some form of drogue or sea anchor. In the absence of either of these – and very few yachts now have them on board – a canvas bucket, even bundled sailbags, bedding etc might serve. The problem here, though, is that these might prove altogether too effective, bringing the boat to an abrupt halt in the water and so allowing the waves to overtake it – with potentially disastrous consequences.

So in the end, there may be nothing for it but to lie a'hull and stow all sails, leaving the boat to its own devices on the basis that it is probably going to adopt the most favourable attitude to the waves without human interference – assuming that at this point the crew are even inclined to interfere. Apart from instilling a feeling of helplessness in the crew, there are arguments against the practice of hulling (though, pragmatically, there may not be all that much choice in the matter).

As with most other things, the ability to lie a'hull with any degree of assured safety depends upon the design of the boat. With all sail stowed, it should settle beam-on to the seas, and in this position both the buoyancy inherent in the topsides and the righting ballast will be at their most effective in preventing a knock-down. However, it could equally well be pointed out

From seaward, the approach to this harbour will appear smooth and relatively unruffled. This photo was taken towards high water, but at low tide, the waves coming in over the shoaling ground will be short and steep. The harbour walls and pilings will create a wind shadow, and possibly severe and unpredictable gusts that will make manoeuvring under sail decidedly dicey.

that this attitude is really that most liable to lead to a knock-down or complete inversion. In reality, yachts are of widely divergent types and the plain truth is that though many will indeed lie beam-on, some will tend to turn and run off down-wind – even with the tiller lashed in an attempt to prevent this; some with excessive windage aft because of a high super-structure (or possibly, a spray hood or cockpit dodgers) may be inclined to weathercock, turning head-to-wind, while the majority of smaller, lighter boats are prone to wandering.

Given a buoyant yacht with adequate ballast ratio, the hull should survive a knock-down (even a complete roll), but the rig might not – and the watertight integrity of ventilators, hatches and windows could well be compromised. Also, there is a high risk of injury to the crew, either from falling displaced objects such as batteries, portable radios and other similar items of equipment, or perhaps by aggravated contact with sharp edges or fastenings in the cabin space; the number of times small boats are seen with a couple of inches of steel machine screw or self-tappers protruding unprotected from the head-lining would suggest that few crews ever take seriously the prospect of severe weather!

With the boat either forereaching very slightly (and a per-formance oriented micro will usually do so to a degree –

whether the crew wish it or not), or drifting to leeward, and riding the waves rather than struggling against them, the possibility of sustaining damage to the rudder is minimised – but it *is* one of the risks attendant upon lying a'hull. Some rudder types are by their nature and construction more delicate than others, but all must be lashed as firmly as possible to prevent movement and possible wringing, especially if the yacht slides backwards (and occasional sternway is to be expected).

Those who strongly favour hulling – often as the primary course of action rather than one forced by necessity – seem on the whole to be sanguine characters bent on fostering the impression that it's all rather fun really: nothing more than whipping the sails off, battening everything down, and retiring with a flask of coffee, a nip of rum and a rattling good book! Yet it is probably fair to say that this reflects the outlook of the individual rather than an accurate assessment of the situation – in other words, it implies a lack of imagination! No doubt about it, lying a'hull can be hard on the crew of any yacht, though the first hour or so below is generally the worst. The motion can be very violent, even where the wind pressure on the rig is sufficient to steady the yacht and maintain a slight angle of heel; this state will at best be intermittent, for in the troughs of waves and temporarily sheltered from the effects of the wind, the yacht will spring upright only to heel again as the following crest takes charge.

Lee cloths will offer but scant protection to the occupants of the berths, and probably the best course of action is to wedge cushions between the main settees, and use blankets, sleeping bags, sails and anything else that is handy to make a secure place in which to doze off on the cabin sole; any prospect of restful slumber while wearing lifejacket, safety harness and oilskins is a bit on the optimistic side, though these are really the preferred apparel for sitting out a blow.

In a well-designed and constructed boat, so long as there are a few square miles of otherwise unoccupied sea, lying a'hull should be safe enough. However, in coastal waters, other shipping will be in the vicinity and, with no sail set, the yacht will be unable to take any form of evasive action – without sails, it will also be more difficult to pick out visually. Especially when tired, there is a temptation for the yacht's crew to assume that an unseen danger is one that can be dismissed; unfortunately, though, larger ships will probably still be trudging on about their business, unperturbed by winds of up to 35 knots and disinclined to reduce speed if there is a need to catch the tide. Therefore a lookout must be maintained, and this means opening the hatch for brief periods. A

Windage
It is easy to underestimate the windage of equipment above deck level: the shaded areas – furled headsail, lowered main and boom, radar reflector, spray cover and dodgers (even the lifebuoy) all combine to add a large leeway component when under storm canvas or lying a'hull.

360 degree scan of the horizon every five to ten minutes will be essential depending on the extent of visibility: waves and flying spray may make it difficult to distinguish anything at a distance. During the hours of darkness, if there are other lights seen in the surrounding area, make an extra attempt to keep a strong white light in the cockpit or illuminating the sails, for when stern-to, a small cruiser will be almost invisible from the bridge or wheelhouse of a vessel bearing down upon it. Check

that white flares are to hand, and that everyone knows how to use them; flares are, after all, explosive devices – and not the tame pyrotechnics associated with many Bonfire night celebrations. It must also be stressed that out-of-date flares are not only unreliable, but can be dangerous if the casings split – so never keep them on board and don't even consider letting them off to enliven a party ashore!

The greatest risk

It will not be easy to estimate wind speeds accurately, but if there was a commercial ship abeam at the time the yacht first lay a'hull and it keeps station through the gale, you've probably sat through a Force 9 gale, ie up to 47 knots of wind! On the other hand, the ship in question might be standing by in case of need – or have got wind of the chance of a nice little salvage claim in the offing; though such renegades are rare, they do exist – so this caution is not quite so paranoid as it may sound!

Being run down is undoubtedly the biggest risk to a yacht lying a'hull, and in waters such as the English Channel, Irish Sea and around Ushant and Finisterre, the crew must be really vigilant. It may sound alarmist, but the crew should face up to the potential hazards of the situation and make provision for survival if the worst does happen and the yacht is holed or sunk. Don't forget that a large vessel may carry on its course, unaware that a collision has occurred.

Assuming that the small cruiser does not carry a liferaft or dinghy, there will still be objects onboard with positive flotation – berth cushions, large empty plastic jerry cans, even fenders, and these should be available for immediate use as additional buoyancy aids. Sailbags or holdalls can each be stuffed with buoyant items along with a watertight torch and staples such as water and chocolate; these individual 'grab bags' can then be sealed at the neck and kept in readiness – though hopefully they will never be needed.

Conceivably, there could be instances where the fact of preparing for an emergency instils a feeling of panic; it should, though, have the opposite effect, giving the crew the sense of being in control of events – for apathy is an enemy to be fought at all costs. If the gale is protracted – few summer gales in our own coastal waters last more than 24 hours or so (though one or more shifts in direction could be expected during that time) – tiredness will tell, so the crew should try to spell each other. Frequently, though, only the skipper of a crew of a small yacht will be experienced, and this really rules out any idea of 'two hours on, two hours off' formal watchkeeping; the best he or she can hope for will be snatched intervals of catnapping, which for some people proves more exhausting than no sleep at all. Yet as well as keeping up the lookout, every effort should be made to plot the dead-reckoning position, even though this may necessarily entail a certain amount of 'guestimation' as to the rate of drift (a rough idea of this can be obtained by observing the behaviour of a buoyant object – perhaps a partially filled plastic container – dropped over the side). If the yacht is equipped with a satellite navigation system, the element of doubt should be removed, but commit everything to paper and keep both the log and charts updated in case the batteries fail or the aerial suffers damage.

From the moment the yacht heaves-to or lies a'hull, everything should be noted down: a change of attitude to the waves, or an increase in their height, perceptible variations in wind strength and direction – all can be used as a back-up by the human computer if the electronics fail!

Be especially vigilant for alterations in the wave pattern that might be indicative of shoals or banks; regular lines of breaking water are easy to see, but the steeper waves caused by converging seas meeting on a bank are difficult to detect (especially in rain or flying spray), and it is these that are potentially so hazardous. 'Rogue waves' are often cited as the cause of otherwise inexplicable losses. Though occasionally dismissed as figments of an over-active imagination, these rogue waves do undoubtedly exist; in coastal waters, they are usually 'reflected waves', which – having struck cliffs or a harbour wall – rebound seawards, travelling fast until colliding with the incoming waves. It is at this point that the combined force of the two systems often give rise to exceptionally steep seas – all the more reason for keeping well clear of land!

Fog

Fog, while generally accompanied by a conspicuous absence of wind, ironically presents the crew with many of the problems of a screaming gale, foremost among these being the need to sit it out until the weather improves. Apart from the problem of seeing (and being seen), there will be difficulty in ascertaining the yacht's whereabouts; after several hours have elapsed, there may be a sense of complete disorientation accompanied by distrust of either the navigator's dead reckoning or the position established by the instruments. Once again, there is also the risk of being run down by

Fog

Keep a good lookout in all directions in fog and remember to look up regularly: in some cases, the fog bank may only be a couple of metres in height and it will be possible to see the superstructure and masts of shipping.

other shipping – radar has merely brought about an increased confidence among the officers on watch, hence such a high incidence of 'radar-assisted' collisions!

If engulfed in fog, however, safety lies in shallow water, usually close inshore, rather than in struggling to gain as much offing as possible (which is the avowed aim if caught in a gale). While drifting (or anchoring) with only a couple of feet of water under the keel is not entirely without risk, it does at least ensure that anything large will run aground before colliding with the yacht. While poor visibility does not necessarily mean that the yacht cannot proceed on passage, this will probably only be feasible under power – so the fuel reserve must be checked before committal to a particular course of action. In home waters, the crew may be certain that they are caught in a localised patch of sea mist rather than extensive fog; and being familiar with tidal sets and the local buoys, they might be content to carry on in what they consider perfect safety. With less experience, seeking shallow water might be preferable, but take great care crossing shipping channels and separation zones. Whichever option is agreed, establishing an immediate position fix is paramount: keep updating the dead reckoning, and use the RDF if there is one. Where the sea bed shows marked depth variations, the echo sounder will be useful as it will be if steering a course along a given underwater contour line. Concentrate on interpreting the tidal atlas and note any fluctuations or gradients in tidal streams; also, bear in mind the possibility of local currents in bays or around headlands.

If navigating from buoy to buoy, check that the one that looms obligingly out of the mist, dead on the nose and right on schedule, is actually the right one (and in familiar waters it is all too easy to assume that this is the case) by approaching it and reading the name! Take notice of the current flow around the buoy; if nothing else, this will confirm the data in the tidal atlas.

Although buoys have sound signals, fog muffles and distorts noise, so the apparent direction of a sound cannot be relied upon. In thick fog, a buoy can all too easily become an object to impact on rather than a reassuring navigation aid! Even worse is to miss the outlying buoys that warn of wrecks – and not all wrecks are long-rusted ships well below the surface. The disused wartime forts that litter some of our coastal waters – in particular, the Thames estuary, North Sea and Solent spring immediately to mind – can be very dangerous indeed for small yachts, as currents in the vicinity generally run very strongly around them, setting a trap from which escape may be difficult. Even on a clear day, it is not advisable to approach closely; the height of the structure gives rise to a wind shadow – literally taking the wind from the sails – while the current sets the boat on to the obstruction. Several of these crumbling citadels of the sea are very large, and consist of a series of linked towers; unsuccessful attempts have been made to demolish others, a number of which have fangs of concrete and steel-reinforced rod projecting at low water. To happen suddenly upon one of these forts in fog, and to find yourself staring up at the ruins, is a salutary experience and one not easily erased from the memory!

Though there may be stirrings of breeze in a fog bank, these will be fitful; so assuming that there is mechanical power, there will be nothing for it but to motor. As in heavy weather, the fuel reserve must be established, with an allowance for use in emergency. Yet running the engine deprives the crew of the sense of hearing: sometimes the only warning of an approaching ship is the beat of the engines, and this may be inaudible over an outboard (and many inboards for that matter). So the engine will have to be run at low revs – and not all are happy with this state of affairs, with some older two-strokes oiling up the plugs. Neither do all inboards respond well to a stop/start regime, though that may be the only safe way to

Not all wrecks marked on charts are those of ships: this is the Sunk Head Tower seen from the deck of the 16 ft (4.8 m) Shoal Waters. At low water, the debris resulting from an unsuccessful demolition attempt is visible, and the baulks of concrete and vicious fangs of the steel reinforcement make the structure even more dangerous to approach than it might appear from this photo. Note the strong current flow and remember that the wreck will create a wind shadow: it would not be difficult to be literally sucked on to the tower and impaled. Keep clear – even in settled weather.

keep way on and still listen out for other vessels. A lookout – if that is the right term for a member of crew upon whose ears rather than eyes the safety of the yacht may depend – should be stationed on the foredeck as far from the noise of the engine as possible. The appropriate sound signals should be made: one long blast of horn or whistle followed by two shorter ones, and this repeated at intervals of not more than two minutes. This may be heard by an alert watchkeeper on a ship's wing bridge, but probably not by two or three souls snug in a wheelhouse with the VHF loudspeaker on!

All the crew should be dressed warmly in layered clothing along with oilskins and lifejackets, and sailing shoes rather than seaboots. Harnesses should be worn, but not clipped on: if there is a collision with a commercial vessel, the best chance of survival lies in being able to swim clear of debris and, supported by a lifejacket, locate buoyant objects (among them hopefully, the emergency 'grab bags') and to regroup. However, in the event of a near miss, the yacht could be thrown bodily to one side by the bow wave of the larger ship, and there will certainly be a few moments of wild and unpredictable rolling in the turbulent aftermath of the wash; thus the crew will need to hook on and hang on for dear life.

Normal recommended procedure is for all those 'off watch' to station themselves on the deck or coachroof, but if the weather is bitter, this strategy should be reassessed: sitting below, close to the companion, will admittedly entail a few seconds' delay in the event of an emergency, but the risk of hypothermia may outweigh this. The decision has to be based on a number of factors: is the yacht in a known shipping lane, or an area much frequented by fishing vessels? Has the look-out reported nearby engine noise? Has anything so far approached dangerously close? This last would suggest that the small yacht gives off little or no radar echo; in this case, one near miss could be followed by another – so remain on deck. Yet for how long? Will it be a matter of hours, or days, before there is a break in the fog?

Though the behaviour of both land and sea fog can, to some extent, be predicted according to the area and time of year in which it occurs, there will always be a margin of error since due allowance must be made for a number of variables – even the tidal streams bringing colder or warmer currents have an effect. A summer land fog that has formed during a cold night over warm ground and then drifted out to sea will probably be burnt off by the heat of the sun by midday; but a sea fog may be of far longer duration and will depend upon the direction of the airflow as well as the temperature to which the air must be cooled in order to condense – the so-called dewpoint. An airstream from warm south-western waters will often have a far higher dewpoint than that of the sea surface around the British shoreline, and the result is fog: fog that as it grows in density and becomes established, tends to grow colder – so becoming self-sustaining and very persistent. Generally, because of surface sea temperatures, in winter and early spring when these are at their lowest, fog forms inshore; and in the summer months with warmer sea temperatures, fog is liable to be encountered further out to sea.

7 Anticipating the Weather

Stay in harbour?

Of course, everyone should know what to do in bad weather and have contingency plans laid and routines perfected, but arguably one of the most important attributes of seamanship is that of *anticipating* adverse conditions – and then steering well clear of them! This poses a vexed question: namely, whether to stay in harbour and miss a favourable breeze because there is warning of a gale 'later' (ie more than 12 hours after the warning's issue), or stay put and be sure of more settled conditions. This is less easy to resolve than might have been the case a few years ago, if only from the point of view of a possible insurance claim. If the yacht meets with an accident, it could be argued that putting to sea in a gale or with an imminent warning (less than six hours) is knowingly endangering the vessel; certainly in recent years there have been claims against race officers who allowed races to proceed in weather that deteriorated to the point where yachts, and lives, were lost.

There is much to be said for remaining in shelter simply because any cruising yacht will encounter quite enough unpleasant weather in the normal course of events without actively seeking it out. This is true enough, but unless practice is acquired in strong-wind sailing, then the experience will be more alarming than it might otherwise be when it does occur. In the end, the decision must be based not only upon the experience (and stamina) of the crew and skipper, but also the boat's intended destination: with a long passage and an offshore summer breeze, a rising wind – so long as it is predicted to remain constant from a favourable quarter – will be a good start to the cruise (though care should be taken that the boat does not save its time on passage only to arrive upon a lee shore with the gale still in force). In winter, don't even consider it – stay in harbour.

Waiting for an assured spell of settled fine weather will mean – in Britain at least – that much of the season may be spent in the home port; but if the crew can understand the weather and interpret signs and portents (be these physical, broadcast or faxed!), they can more confidently plan the cruising itinerary.

Our forebears' economy (and their lives too) depended upon accurate observations of the weather, and there is a good deal of wisdom in the old predictive rhymes: 'red sky at night', 'wind before rain' etc. Such examples are numerous, and it would really need a whole book to collate them.

Books on weather lore are fascinating, but it is to the radio that most sailors now turn for information – usually to the shipping forecasts and updated gale warnings put out by the BBC. Though few smaller yachts are likely to have one, there are facsimile printers with information issuing from shore-based radio transmitters. These are very useful, but watching a gale warning materialise in cold print can send a shiver down the spine – even advance notification of an imminent Force 10 sounds more reassuring when delivered in the calm and unemotional tones of a BBC announcer!

Heavy rain and gale force winds are associated with depressions; these troughs of low pressure, though deriving from warm and cold air masses in collision, are really the end product of numerous complex interactions between the earth's pressure belts, global wind systems, the surface temperatures of oceans and land masses, and also the presence of evaporating and condensing water vapour – the stuff of which clouds are made. And one of the indications of the weather to come is in cloud formations. Not of course that any sort of accurate prediction can be based upon clouds alone: the barometer is indispensable – and really ranks next to the compass in order of importance. (Often, though, when equipping a small cruiser, this is one purchase that is overlooked.)

All of those who sail should be acquainted with the weather – not only of the developing systems, but also of certain wind patterns liable to be encountered in the cruising area; wind funnelling down over a hilly coastline will, close inshore, give rise to strong breezes blowing out to sea and often contrary to those forecast. In fiords and inlets such as those of the northern coast of Spain and the Western Isles of Scotland, exceptionally vicious blasts can be encountered, virtually without any prior warning. Though these are most dangerous to an open boat or sailing dinghy, the crew of a small yacht can expect to find themselves quite preoccupied until the squall eases off!

Weather patterns

Even with the aid of satellites and weather radar, forecasting is still far from an exact science, although predictions can be made with a greater degree of success than was formerly the case. Perhaps the most noticeable difference is in the medium term. In our coastal waters, conditions rarely remain stable for very long – and weather systems travel fast – but even so, over a six-hour period, a great deal of additional information will be gained from observing barometric changes and also cloud formations and movements.

First of all, clouds have to be identified, and this is not always quite so straightforward as photos in reference books might suggest. With the exception of the broad streets of fair-weather cumulus marching towards the distant horizon, clouds merge: scud – fragmented storm cloud – can form in wisps that easily get confused with cirrus, and, to further confuse the issue, high-, medium- and low-altitude clouds may also appear to overlap. When making notes of broadcast information, and barometric pressure in the immediate and adjoining sea areas, drawing up a basic weather map is often suggested. If there is time to spare, it can be interesting to sketch cloud formations as well, for this helps to train the eye.

On peering through the hatch, the first thing that can be seen is the amount of cloud cover, even if this does little more than confirm earlier suspicions. The next and easiest distinction is usually between high and low cloud, and the high cirrus – whose mare's tails trail in feathered banners, appearing to converge on the horizon – is easily picked out. This has long been regarded as the precursor of bad weather, and since it is generally a pre-frontal cloud, this does tend to be true – with strong winds pretty well guaranteed when lower cumulus clouds can be seen blowing across the cirrus.

Cirro-stratus is composed of ice crystals, and is thin, vaguely defined, a hazy drift across the whole sky, though it may still be possible to see the sun or moon – assuming that there is no low altitude cloud to obscure them. It is cirro-stratus that gives rise to the characteristic halo around the moon: yet another time-honoured prediction, and another that is fairly accurate, for the high thin cloud will gradually thicken into a grey veil of alto-stratus and so warn of an approaching trough. (This may then thicken yet again to form nimbo-stratus with rain and strengthening winds.)

Last – but least significant so far as forecasting is concerned – is cirro-cumulus cloud, whose dappled striations have caused it to be known as the 'mackerel sky'; this, in

British waters at least, has an ill-deserved reputation as a herald of deteriorating conditions.

Much can be gained from a correct interpretation of clouds at a lower altitude, though here too definitions may blur. The cloud of dull days – too many of them in our coastal waters – is stratus; this is formless, depressingly grey, often thick enough to obscure sun or moon, and a backdrop for other clouds. Yet even the cumulus associated with fine weather and summer days can differ in portent according to size: large cumulus (cumulo-nimbus), which towers skywards for literally thousands of feet, can produce sudden and heavy showers of rain and is likely to develop into the so-called anvil-topped formations indicative of thunderstorms. If rain is falling, this causes violent downdrafts of air that will result in gusts – gusts capable of decimating a racing fleet – or even dismasting an unprepared cruiser. Here, you will have only the evidence of your eyes to warn you: squalls will be sudden, and the barometer is, for once, unlikely to give much prior indication.

Depressions, while occurring more frequently in the winter months, can also form in summer; they are often short-foretold and short-lived (another old maxim well proven), yet these summer storms can wreak havoc. The trough can move in any direction, but normally tracks east to north-east – though a minority arrive from the east and edge south across the British Isles. So far as forecasting goes, much depends upon where the depression first forms; if the starting point is close, there will be less prior indication than if a depression is moving slowly – having formed several hundred miles away.

Swell, building up in advance of strengthening wind and moving outwards from the centre of the trough, is another intimation of a gale to come; the swell, however, may be indistinguishable from the wave system. The barometer will fall, possibly after an earlier small rise, and cloud will thicken. These signs will, along with radio forecasts, help to establish the time remaining before the gale does strike, and also its duration and the probable direction of subsequent wind shifts. This is vital information when deciding upon a strategy, ie whether to make for harbour or gain an offing.

8   Basic Essentials

Planning the summer cruise must be counted as one of the great pleasures of winter, but there is no escaping the fact that fitting even a small yacht for the sea is a costly undertaking. Although many items can be bought second-hand from private individuals, or boat jumbles and auctions, quality still has to be paid for.

Every vessel, be it maxi racer or micro cruiser, has to be equipped for the conditions that it is liable to encounter, whether on a coastal passage or ocean crossing. For the small yacht, the major constraint must inevitably be that of stowage space; there is very little room to spare for non-essential items – indeed, there may be hardly sufficient space for those items essential to the safe running of the yacht.

The ground tackle

Excess weight should also be avoided. In the smallest and lightest boats, if heavy gear is concentrated in the stern, performance in light airs will suffer – noticeably so if a broad transom is so deeply immersed that it increases drag; put too much weight forward, and the boat will bury the bows in a chop. Yet, while accepting this fact, there should be no attempt to minimise weight by cutting down on the size of anchor and chain: here, avoirdupois must be secondary to safety, and the ground tackle is the one instance where extra weight for its own sake is indispensable rather than merely justifiable!

Unfortunately, in spite of the fact that attention is constantly drawn to the need for anchors and chain to be of a size appropriate to an individual vessel, in practice it is rare for the small yacht (rarer still for the small cruiser) to carry a bower anchor of anything approaching the correct weight or, for that matter, sufficient scope of good-quality short-link tested chain. As for a kedge anchor – don't bother to enquire! This is hard to understand, for no cruising boat can ever be certain of dropping the hook each time in a sheltered anchorage with good holding ground; indeed, in recent years, anchoring anywhere, at any time, seems to have gone out of fashion – at least, that is the impression given by those boatbuilders who apparently are convinced that small modern yachts only daysail from mooring

Left *A neat foredeck well with a strong sampson post for mooring. Chafe on a mooring could be reduced by the provision of twin stemhead rollers, one each side of the short bowsprit.*

Right *Another good foredeck well with carefully positioned cleats and leads. Note the double stemhead roller fair to the centreline bollard, which is better suited to chain than are cleats. A navel pipe is sited to starboard, and the warp and chain are stowed below decks.*

to marina, lying to a pontoon, berthing alongside, or rafting up for a quick dash to the pub!

This gives an excuse for what could be called the minimalist approach: it has now become commonplace to fit mooring cleats that are highly polished and elegantly streamlined, but quite undersized – and manifestly unsuitable for use with chain (a good solid sampson post or cruciform bollard really is essential). Fortunately, stemhead rollers are still 'in', but these too seem to be pale imitations of their former selves and are not infrequently supplanted by ingenious fitments incorporating a rope channel, the forestay attachment, pulpit and everything else bar an attachment for taking stones from horses' hooves (if any section suffers damage, the entire fabrication has to be removed for repair!). And most sinister of all, the navel pipe has now become obsolete. This in itself would not matter – stowing the cable on deck within a purpose-moulded anchor well or locker in the foredeck admittedly keeps weed and mud out of the forepeak where its presence can be quite pervasive – especially if the ground tackle was not scrubbed prior to stowage. It is also true that with a navel pipe it is hard to eliminate that trickle of water that persistently finds its way below.

However, while carrying anchor and chain on deck may be acceptable (if not ideal) on a 30 ft (9.1 m) heavy displacement cruiser, so far as the average micro yacht goes it would be hard to think of a worse place to lug around a hundredweight of iron and steel – which is what the correctly sized anchor for a 20 ft (6 m) yacht, together with a minimum 15 fathoms of chain, will indeed weigh. And since most sailors are quite aware that a locker well above the waterline and in the eyes of the boat is not a sensible place for carrying chain – they don't, and opt instead to replace chain with rope! But, this really is not satisfactory for a serious cruising yacht of any size. Because of its weight, chain sinks, at once exerting a pull on the anchor that is close to horizontal, helping the anchor to bite quickly and then to dig ever deeper into the sea bed. It is also far stronger, resistant to chafe, and not likely to be cut by a propeller or severed deliberately by vandals – both of which occurrences are far from unknown. Against this, it cannot of course be cut free should this become necessary; therefore ensure that the bitter end (attached to a strong point below) is made fast by a rope tail that can be sliced through instantly. By all means, use a length of chain and warp on the kedge (and do carry a kedge), but not on the main anchor – even though this will involve the fitting of a chainpipe and stowage bin below decks. One other good thing about chain, though, is that it stacks itself neatly and, unlike rope, does not have to be laboriously coiled or flaked down after use.

Anchors tend to be acquired along with the yacht, so the size and type may not be questioned by new owners. However, it is fair to say that these anchors are often too small. There are several means of calculating the right weight of anchor for each boat, but a reasonable guideline – one that is biased towards safety – is to allow 1 lb (0.4 kg) of anchor weight per foot of the yacht's waterline length, then add 10 per cent for the bower anchor, and subtract 10 per cent for the kedge.

Anchor types vary considerably as regards holding power-to-weight ratios, though undoubtedly the effectiveness of different designs differs according to the nature of the sea or river bed. The plough is often regarded as the best for all-round use, with the Danforth possibly having a slight edge in mud. (This type is very simply made up by amateur metal workers, so beware the fakes seen at boat jumbles; as with any anchor, only buy a known branded type, and one in first-class condition.) The Bruce is claimed to have excellent holding in just about any surface and has the advantage of stowing neatly over the stem, which possibly accounts for its popularity with small yachts. The fisherman type is less favoured by yachtsmen, partly because of the ease with which it is fouled by other lines (or indeed its own); but as it will nearly always get some sort of grip even in rock crevices or thick growths of kelp, it just might save a boat in danger of driving onshore. Grapnels (with four flukes) are rarely used now except by dinghies, and rond anchors, with only one fluke, are designed for catching a hold in reed beds or hooking on to banks. Mushroom types, employed mainly for permanent mud moorings, also rarely feature in a yacht's inventory!

The holding power of a smaller anchor can be increased by sliding a weight down the chain or warp; this will improve the angle of lie, and so make for a more effective pull. Another handy addition to the ground tackle of even a small yacht (supposing there is room) is a light 'lunch hook'; this is just what the name implies: an anchor of perhaps 8–10 lb (3.6–4.5 kg) in weight that can be used when mooring for an hour or so in settled weather. It will be quick to clean and stow afterwards – and capable of being recovered by even the junior crew members.

Mooring warps and fenders should not be the subject of an economy drive either. Bulky though fenders are, you will not begrudge the stowage space they occupy if you make a habit of mooring in crowded harbours – a small yacht is rarely left to lie in peace for long; due to its size, it will be edged to the outside of the trot by larger craft. If the crew have been so misguided as to nip ashore for a quick one, their boat may suffer at the hands (or more probably, the bows) of incoming boats, some of which are bound to have a laid-back approach to the topsides of smaller yachts – which may be regarded as a useful, if rather less resilient, sort of fender!

Unfortunately, any pretence of good manners has, in some harbours at least, been thrown to the winds. Ten years or so ago, no one (well no one in a state of sobriety) would dream of marching roughshod through the cockpit of a neighbouring yacht or over the coachroof of a populated vessel; neither would they blast heavy metal through cockpit speakers until all hours – but now they do! Equally, common courtesy once dictated enquiries from newcomers as to who intended to be

first away in the morning, and warps taken to the quay would
be made fast accordingly; these days, in contrast, it is not
uncommon to find a couple of 10 tonners rafted up without
springs and breast ropes (or any lines to the shore), and made
fast only to the mooring cleats of adjoining boats – regardless
of size!

Electrical power on board

The tools of the navigator's trade are, if nothing else, compact;
still, the choice of aids for the small yacht may be rather limited, though this will more often be down to the ship's electrical system rather than available space.

An increasing number of small craft now have satellite,
Decca, or even GPS navigation systems. The price of these has
reduced in real terms over the years, and the simplified
smaller units – although not without occasional glitches – are
increasingly reliable and economical to install; and if the
yacht is sold, they can easily be removed if required. Yet,
whichever is chosen (and it does seem as though GPS will in
the end reign supreme if only because of the vast defence
budget that can be pretty well guaranteed to maintain it), all
require a regular supply of current that is free from fluctuations – such as might be caused by engine starting, etc. For
this reason, a separate battery, independently charged, is
advisable.

If the yacht has a fairly recent inboard engine, there will in
all probability be an alternator fitted, and this will reliably
charge the 12 volt batteries generally used for the electrical
system of a small vessel; however, there are some early
engines with dynamos that can best be described as erratic,
and whose output cannot be counted upon – even when the
engine is revving quite hard. Outboards may be fitted with a
lighting coil providing enough power for navigation and
domestic lights, but all means of engine charging are of course
dependent upon the engine running for a sufficient length of
time – and this may not always be convenient.

In the end, it comes down to a matter of priorities: a small
yacht that is intending to cruise at night, and to make use of
instruments and an autopilot, will need at least one heavy-
duty battery; if it is impractical to charge this by the yacht's
engine, alternatives must be considered – the 'green' options
being a wind charger (which will certainly do nothing for the
yacht's performance under sail due to its high drag component) or photovoltaics (solar panels). These, consisting of sili-

con cells, wired in series and 'drifting' under the influence of light, can, depending on size, produce an output of 5–60 watts. Although the output will vary slightly according to light intensity, strong sunlight is no longer needed to produce a current. Neither are the panels as fragile as they once were; those designed for small yachts are laminated without glass and can also be curved to accommodate the camber of deck or coachroof. However, inevitably the size will be restricted, and therefore solar panels must be regarded as a secondary 'top-up' system if the yacht's electrics have a high current drain.

Clearly, then, other means of charging must be found – the most obvious one being to plug into shore power at a marina and make one or more overnight stops part of the cruise schedule. The second alternative is to hire a portable generator; this is not expensive – at the time of writing, about £15 for the first day and a negligible sum for any subsequent days (and I have, more than once, recouped the cost by doing the rounds of a boatyard, charging batteries at a fiver a go!). Indeed, one of these units is so useful that it is worth considering its outright purchase, and the smallest models will fit neatly beneath the cockpit sole or bridgedeck bulkhead. They require very little fuel, but they do need ventilation in use and should not be operated in the cabin.

With an inboard engine and an alternator for battery charging, it might seem as though the problem is resolved – but ironically, the engine itself can be one of the most conspicuous consumers of current; if fitted with electric starting, the drain when the engine is initially turned over is considerable (particularly in the case of a diesel with its high compression); and to make certain of an adequate reserve of power, a twin-battery system ought to be fitted. The batteries should be wired in parallel with a simultaneous trickle charge, and fitted with a changeover switch that allows either one or both to be used for engine starting and for domestics. (This also ensures that in the event of a failure of the first battery, it cannot discharge the second.) Twelve volt batteries are unfortunately rather heavy objects, and should therefore be positioned as low as possible in the yacht – but clear of any bilge water that might accumulate in normal conditions; nearly all small yachts do get a bit of spray below under way, and some leak even on a mooring! The batteries must be securely strapped so as to stay put no matter what (and this would include possible inversion of the yacht) and be sited in a vented box. If they are taken ashore for charging, it makes sense to fit rope-carrying handles to the box and remove each unit in its entirety.

The low-tech alternatives

Many of those sailing small craft favour the 'low-tech' option and keep everything as simple as possible, holding steadfastly to the opinion that electrics and water don't mix – and even on larger yachts, where the equipment and batteries can be protected from the elements and all-pervasive damp of a marine environment and instruments integrated into purpose-built joinery, there still remains an element of truth in this belief. This being so, anyone planning a long passage or cruising to remote areas would be well advised to have comprehensive back-up systems.

Whether the small cruiser actually needs electrics, other than for navigation lights, is open to question, since almost without exception the functions of electronics can be duplicated mechanically – or, if absolutely necessary, manually! A lead line may be more laborious in use than an echo sounder, but it works (and, if the hollow in the lead is armed with tallow, also provides information about the nature of the sea bed), while a buoyant object thrown overboard from the bows can be timed as it passes astern to give a fair idea of the speed through the water.

Neither is there any need for an electronic autopilot (which, when earning its keep in rough going or with a headstrong boat, uses more current than you might be led to believe), since mechanical wind vane systems are widely available, and range from the super-sophisticated to the most basic.

The best (not necessarily the most expensive) will steer just about any yacht on any point of sailing, although none are all that effective in very light winds. As far as construction goes, the majority of those produced commercially are pretty rugged; they are, after all, built with ocean crossings in mind. However, with strength are associated size and weight; and therefore some, such as the very well-engineered 'Aries' gear, would not be suitable for the small cruiser. Even one of the smaller gears such as the French 'Capeole' would require a substantial mounting bracket – difficult to construct so as not to mar the appearance of a small yacht, especially one with pronounced retroussé stern.

Self-steering gears

Self-steering gears operate in a variety of ways in order to achieve the same object: namely, reliability on a par with a competent human helmsman. Keep in mind, though, that the

Self-steering system with horizontal vane and servo rudder on this world-girdling micro. Coloured Terylene sails, though, are not recommended for such prolonged exposure to ultraviolet light as they rapidly degrade.

vane will steer the yacht in accordance with wind shifts, so the position must regularly be checked with the compass heading; if it is not, after a few hours' fast sailing, the vessel could deviate miles from the intended course.

The sensing vane may swivel in the vertical plane, as does the early Hasler, or it can pivot horizontally as with the Hydrovane gear. The vane will, in turn, activate either (i) a rudder that is a separate appendage from the yacht's main rudder, or (ii) a trim tab mounted on the trailing edge of main rudder, or (iii) the most powerful of all, a pendulum or servo blade that pivots on its horizontal axis, exerting a downward pressure in a similar way to that applied when sculling.

The simplest gear of all, that devised by Pete Beard, uses a horizontally pivoting vane that acts directly on steering lines to the tiller. Apart from being very simple (and economical), it works remarkably well – and is well suited to a small cruiser in that it can be mounted on a pushpit or quarter stanchion and, to one side, clear of a transom-hung rudder.

All of the commercially manufactured gears have their enthusiasts who will not hear a word against them. Having had an unpleasant experience with one of the better-known types when the tiller chains jammed at what could best be termed a critical moment, I prefer a system that leaves the tiller free and acts instead upon an independent rudder: with the vane locked, this can serve as emergency steering should the yacht's main rudder suffer damage.

All transom-mounted gears are vulnerable to damage in harbour, and can also inflict damage on others, so they need to be fitted with some form of protection. There is always the possibility of hitting an underwater obstruction, so the blade or pendulum must kick up on impact (or a shear pin be fitted).

Structural failure can occur too; many units rely partially upon cast aluminium and this can crack or fracture – though this is rare. However, if buying a self-steering system second-hand, be wary if it has not been seen in action. Without the original handbook or specialised knowledge, it is hard to establish whether the system is intact. With older types, manufacturer's spares will be unobtainable and have to be custom-made.

Long before the advent of mechanical aids, it was discovered that by altering the set of the sails – or by adding small auxiliary ones – many sailing vessels could be persuaded to sail, under certain conditions, without a·human hand on the tiller. Joshua Slocum's assertion that his circumnavigating *Spray* could steer itself aroused considerable disbelief, but the secret of using a small jigger on a mizzen mast was already well known to the Thames barge crews. (*Gypsy Moth III*'s vane was really a small mizzen rather than a vane as such.)

Although neither the hulls nor the gaff rig of yachts at the turn of the century made it easier to coerce a yacht to self-steer, most modern yachts can usually be counted on to do so (at least on the wind), although in the case of lightweight micros, the sensitivity to weight and the designers' liking of imbalanced ends that cause the centre of buoyancy to shift excessively as the angle of heel steepens makes this a delicate operation. Ideally, a hull should possess good directional stability, and a degree of weather helm is helpful too – not, however, too much.

Assuming that the yacht fulfils these criteria, self-steering by sail trim should call for no more than lines, shock-cord and perseverance. The principle is simple: sail area abaft the rig's centre of effort pushes the head up to the wind while the area forward has precisely the opposite effect, pushing down to leeward. With headsail backed a little, the boat should keep a steady course, although slowing slightly; this is easy to achieve, even though it could be argued that the boat is to all intents and purposes hove-to rather than steering a course on the wind. On a reach, in order to maintain acceptable forward progress, more fiddling is called for: the foresail has to be sheeted so that the turning moment produced exactly matches that of the rudder. So, a rubber strop is made fast from the lee side and the sail sheeted via a block on to the weather side of the tiller. As the boat bears off, the sail will stall, lose drive and so ease the tension on the sheet. The main will then blanket the foresail and so increase its own power; the tiller is pulled to leeward and the boat luffs to resume the original course. It takes patience and some experimentation with sail areas, but is quite effective. (This is an accomplishment well worth mastering, as the boat can be steered simply by sail trim should the rudder be lost or severely damaged.) On a dead run, twin-boomed staysails with sheets led directly to the tiller can also be used; the principle is essentially similar: as one sail loses power, so its neighbour acquires it – ad infinitum!

Electronic logs – those favoured by yachts being either the impeller or paddlewheel type – are accurate and trouble free, although weed and marine growth do adversely affect the efficiency. However, many serious cruising people still remain faithful to the patent mechanical type; certainly the trailing log is well tried, having been in use since the nineteenth century. These have earned rather a reputation for under-reading in light airs, but this can often be attributed to a tow line being too long. It is this line, used to tow the rotator or 'fish' astern, that is the one drawback to a fitting that is, in other respects, first rate, simple, reasonably priced and easy to demount and stow when not in use. Lines are so easy to forget when coming into harbour under power (or when trolling for mackerel), and also require care when handing at the end of a cruise. Detach the line at the register end first, allow it to go overboard, then – hand over hand – bring in the rotator – failure to do it this way will result in a snake's nest of kinks and twists! Rotators often fall victim to predatory fish, snapping at what they perceive to be an attractive lure; indeed, no self-respecting blue water yacht ever completes a passage without losing at least one in this way – it adds to 'sea cred'! A rather more mundane explanation is that the majority fall victim to floating debris rather than denizens of the deep.

The compass

The compass, as with the ground tackle, is often purchased along with the new boat, and many owners are perfectly satisfied with the instrument supplied. Equally, though, there are those prepared to pay a good deal of money for a top-class compass, and the best ones are expensive. Over the years, they transfer this instrument from boat to boat with them. It is

A compass adjuster checking for heeling error – this can be quite pronounced on sailing craft.

important for the card to be clearly marked and to move freely so that it can be read at all times, but not all modern compasses fulfil these criteria. The porthole variety, sometimes mounted in pairs to port and starboard on the accommodation bulkhead, are fine for racing and tactical sailing, but at night or in rain they are not the easiest to read. (It can be difficult to adjust them so that they agree as well!) Probably the best for the smaller vessel is a grid type, with a good-sized horizontal card; this can be sited either on a cockpit thwart, the lower flushing board, or wherever suits the helmsman best – so long, of course, as there is nothing in the vicinity that can cause deviation. This can be a problem in small yachts simply because everything inevitably winds up cheek by jowl with everything else. It is also easy to overlook items that may have an effect: an outboard (or inboard) under the cockpit sole or steel fuel tanks; and of course radio speakers, cameras and tools can all cause deviation. The electronics too can have an effect, though a safe installation distance is generally marked (if not, consult the manufacturers) and the magnetic head of an autopilot is another likely culprit. Incidentally, the fact that there is a timber or GRP bulkhead between the compass and the ferrous object is irrelevant. Larger cruising yachts do often have the compass professionally adjusted; smaller ones rarely do, even though the heeling error may be more pronounced.

Most navigators carry a hand-bearing compass – although it has to be said that using one aboard a small yacht is far less easy than is made out since the sails and rigging tend to obstruct sight lines. Any sort of sea complicates matters still further; bearings will only be obtainable when cresting waves and therefore accuracy may be doubtful – it takes a fair bit of skill and experience to aim the compass accurately whilst managing to retain a secure handhold. Remember too that galvanised rigging can affect the compass reading.

There are several models of handbearing compass available, including those incorporated in lightweight binoculars. Even disregarding price – and bearing binoculars are very pricey – people do have strong personal preferences, some swearing by the small, tough models which fit easily into the palm of the hand, others preferring larger, heavier models with an attached handle. The larger types have clearer and steadier cards but they may prove more difficult to stow. Try to borrow different models, to use at sea before making a final decision. The best aids to navigation must be regarded as an excellent investment as, of course, must each and every item of safety equipment.

Safety equipment

There should be suitable, in-date fire extinguishers in each cabin and to hand in the cockpit. A fire blanket is also required for the galley, but make sure that the crew know how to use it; practise with a fabric square on an unlit stove. The instructions on the apparatus will be clear but it takes a firm resolve to go close enough to a fire to smother it.

Automatic fire extinction is usually recommended in the case of an inboard engine; this is straightforward to fit and relatively inexpensive. However, some people are opposed to these because of the chance of an accidental discharge due to a sensor malfunctioning.

This complaint is also levelled at other warning devices and unfortunately no smoke alarm or gas detector is 100 per cent reliable and the crew may lose confidence in one prone to overreact, often switching it off or, in extremis, depositing it in the yard skip. One thing, though, is certain: where operation is manual, all the crew (including the younger members) must be shown how to use the equipment. Neither fire nor flood will wait for an adult to return on board after a shopping trip ashore!

The same holds true for safety procedures such as 'man

overboard' drill; every possible course of action should be discussed and practised. This does tend to give everyone, even the less experienced, a sense of purpose and working together rather than being mere passengers. All those on board should also be responsible for their personal lifejackets and harnesses (even if borrowed) and tools such as pliers, knife and torch.

The dinghy

The sort of dinghy that is best for a small yacht is yet another subject upon which opinions vary: there are some who resolutely refuse to row in the conviction that the Good Lord gave us outboards so that such exertion could be avoided; with this attitude, an inflatable would be the automatic choice as it would not matter that these are not at their best under oars in a wind-over-tide chop. Although an inflatable is at first thought the most practical tender for the micro yacht, the decision is not actually so straightforward as it initially seems. True, an inflatable from a reputable manufacturer has the great advantage of being almost unsinkable and will withstand astonishing punishment. Inflatables are also stable – except perhaps when it comes to the matter of boarding the yacht from the dinghy; an air-filled centre thwart provides an indifferent foothold; with the exception of a minority of badly designed and cranky GRP examples, most rigid dinghies are steadier. A 7 ft 6 in to 8 ft (2.2–2.4 m) timber or GRP dinghy, will, if towed astern, slow a small yacht, but on the other hand an inflatable is unhappy under tow and cannot be guaranteed to remain rightside up in anything but a gentle swell. And if a rigid dinghy cannot be carried on the coachroof of a micro – well, neither can an inflatable unless it is at least partly deflated (and in this case, it cannot be launched in a hurry). True, an inflatable is kinder to topsides, but an evening spent attaching coir rope or rubber fendering will soften the impact from a rigid dinghy quite effectively.

I am afraid I rather mistrust dinghies that fold since I still have a clear recollection of foundering (in front of the clubhouse – where else?) in one of the early Prout Scoprels. Yet there were some surprisingly good designs, costly though they were (and are); one that originated in France had a heavy rubberised fabric skin with ash frames and longerons. It didn't look good, but was a delight to handle – although only after risking a hernia during the assembly operation! (And who can forget the 'Leakey' (sic) folding boat; it was well made, and doubtless is now marketed by someone who blessed it with a more fortunate choice of name.) However, folding dinghies, although light and easy to carry on deck, always seem a bit fragile for serious family transport. Ideally, a dinghy should be stable, easy to row, and with positive buoyancy. Returning after a weekend afloat to find the dinghy sunk on the mooring is hardly the perfect end to a cruise! (Inflatables, though, are remarkably easy to steal when ashore: even children can pick one up and trot off with it – and the chances of identification and recovery are not good.)

Human resources

However, even the best-equipped yacht (large or small) is still dependent upon what the business world now refers to as 'human resources' – in other words, the crew.

Not altogether surprisingly, people discover that being in a confined space for just one weekend can be quite stressful, and not even families necessarily coexist in perfect harmony. Daysailing with friends may not show up the personality traits that can so easily grate after spending a longer period on board: some people will exist quite contentedly in astonishing squalor, while others cringe at the sight of an unplumped cushion; there are those who'll scoff junk food from the packet or tin, while there are those who insist on three meals daily – and not just meals, but epicurean delights, elaborately served at the same time each day. Some relish a quiet evening in the cockpit with a mug of cocoa watching the sunset, while others are hell bent on finding the nearest disco and fast-food joint. It is such a pity that so often such complete opposites are con-demned to spending a holiday in each other's company.

Before embarking on the summer cruise, it is sensible to have a trial weekend together to find out whether or not you are going to get along; and to discover likes and dislikes so that, assuming everyone still remains on speaking terms after-wards, the cruise can be planned to cater as far as possible for all preferences. And there will of course be individual weak-nesses and strengths: one person may be nervous of night sail-ing (or have less than perfect night vision); one may be safely left on the helm in a Force 6, with heavy sea and wind dead aft; another may be an inspired trimmer of the spinnaker, but useless on the helm – and so on. There is no point in turning an enjoyable cruise into an endurance test for the sake of it, so try to meet people's various needs as far as is possible.

The crew depend upon the micro yacht and its equipment

for their enjoyment, and possibly even their survival; equally, the boat is dependent upon the crew – and nowhere is the old maxim that a happy crew is an efficient one more true than on a small boat. It is, however, just as true to say that there are few types of more rewarding sailing than on a small boat with a crew who have become friends; and this must surely be one reason why so many who first put to sea in micros stay faithful to them for a lifetime of sailing.

Index